CUTTING TIES

CUTTING TIES

Healing from Betrayal Trauma
as the Spouse of an Addict

ROXANNE KENNEDY

CUTTING TIES: Healing from Betrayal Trauma as the Spouse of an Addict ©2018 by Roxanne Kennedy

Printed in the United States of America.

ISBN: 978-1-942707-92-9
Library of Congress Control Number: 2018956940

Cover photography and design by Curtis Bingham.
Edited by Becky Harding, Geoff Steurer, & Leann Coleman.

Forthefaithofit@gmail.com
www.CuttingTies.com
Instagram: cuttingties_book
Facebook: @RKennedyCuttingTies

 Published by Silver Torch Press
www.SilverTorchPress.com
Jill@SilverTorchPress.com

Table of Contents

INTRODUCTION

Two days after a life-changing experience that you will read about in the first chapter, I was on the treadmill thinking through what had happened and how I got to this place. There in my mind, as if I was actually physically seeing it, the cover of the book was shown to me. I saw the title, the image, and the colors. Shocked, I questioned God in my mind, "Am I writing a book?"

As the words flowed through me, the first chapter was written, as God told me, *"Yes, please write this book. Share your heartache, your growth, and your faith. The world needs truth."*

Trauma is universal. Everyone experiences it in some form, some more than others, but there is no one exempt from heartbreak. With this commission to write, I felt a bit confused and shocked as I had not written a book before. I didn't know this was even possible. Yet I saw the cover, the title, and the first chapter as it sped through my brain in a few short minutes. With that, I accepted the challenge.

Each time I sat down to write, I said a prayer before I got started. I didn't want any of the words to come solely from me. Heavenly Father asked me to write this book and in return I asked Him to give me the words. So I sat down, turned on the computer, said a prayer, and waited.

In the prayer, I would say, "If I'm supposed to write today, give me the words." I couldn't stress and worry about what to say, or if I was saying the right things. I didn't need an extra burden in my life. Plus, Satan liked to tell me I wasn't good enough or qualified to write. And I hated hearing that! It was hard for me not to believe him. Because it's partly true. I'm not a writer. Well, I *wasn't* a writer. But Heavenly Father has shown me a new gift. He's given me new light, wisdom, and perspective with this trial. And because He is showing me something new, He stands with me to do it. I am not alone trying to fumble my way through.

If God wanted me to write, He would tell me. And there has not been a time yet that I wasn't given the subject and words within a matter of seconds after the close of my prayer.

He is guiding me because He knows that the things He has taught me, and the things I have gone through, can be of support to you. He knows of your pain and wants to offer you validation as well as hope and understanding that there is a purpose in going through hard things. He does not leave us alone in this. He offers His love and comfort. He gives us resources to build upon. Those new insights get us through to the next step.

I'm grateful for all God has taught me through this heart-breaking and heart-building trial. I'm glad I have been blessed to share it with you. I didn't do any of this perfectly, as you will read. I fumbled my way through, just as we all do. I am here today because I chose to fumble my way through with God by my side. Whatever you have faced, are currently enduring, or will be challenged with, I hope you will feel the message of this book and know that you are not alone. If you are suffering, there are many others sharing your pain and dealing with the same kinds of things. Whether addiction-related or not, there are always others that can understand our pain and trials.

Throughout the book I talk about crazy-making. This shows in my writing. The thinking back and forth is how it feels when a spouse of an addict is trying to make sense of their world. We are constantly searching our mind for what is real, what is true, and what are lies. As you are jumping between past and present, notice that chaos, and you will have an understanding of the crazy-making I reference.

This book was mainly written between the fall of 2014 and July 2015. I was in the middle of so many decisions and in waiting. Often times, I felt compelled to write during some very trying times. Addiction or any other mental illness feels crazy. I wrote when I felt chaotic and filled with stress and anxiety. You will experience almost as if in real time how it felt right along with me. So hang on for the ride. My main goal was to share the painful truth and that, with work and effort, healing and peace are possible for all of us. It takes time, but it can happen if you want it. I am blessed to share my life with you. My intent is for you to feel all the love, faith, and hope I felt as I wrote.

XOXO Roxanne Kennedy
Forthefaithofit@gmail.com

CHAPTER 1

My Life Became Unmanageable

I hurried into our closet, huffing and growling under my breath, trying to hold back the tears, repeating over and over, "Oh, my gosh. Oh, my gosh."

I grabbed the sides of my face with both hands.

"I don't know what to do!"

I was breathing so loud and heavy I thought I might hyperventilate. I was in serious mental trouble. I was distraught and angry. My eyes squeezed shut and my head thrashed from side to side. I felt confused. It was apparent that my life had become unmanageable. For a split second, I opened my eyes, looked up, and there they were…all nicely in a row, so organized and hanging at eye level. At that moment, I knew exactly what I wanted to do.

I wanted to cut them. That's all I wanted to do. It's as if they were mocking me, laughing in my face reminding me of all that I didn't have and all that was wrong with this perfectly organized life. There they hung, over the closet bar, completely even, color coordinated, nothing out of place. I grabbed some scissors that, luckily, or maybe sadly, were within reach. I cut and cut and cut. They were a tiny pair with no more than a two-inch blade. I could have stopped. It wasn't a quick, easy job. But I kept going. With each cut I poured my hate, anger, and fear through my hands to force this perfection into upheaval.

With a sigh of relief, I was done. I breathed out. It felt good. I felt satisfied. Then something else happened. I noticed I also felt more hate and more betrayal. Although that was a release of all that I couldn't control, I also felt so very broken. I fell to the floor and sobbed. My soul felt crushed, and I didn't know at that moment how I was possibly going to heal and become whole.

I left. I filled my overnight bag with two days' worth of clothes and walked out. I prayed aloud.

I yelled, "I am so broken! Can't you see I've had enough?"

All I wanted was for God to see this craziness and say, *"Whoa, she has hit rock bottom."* Couldn't He say, *"You've done all you could and more, and I'm telling you now that you can leave him and start a new life. I'm proud of you and all you have done, but you are now let off the hook."* Couldn't He just say that?

No, that's not what He said. Instead I felt these impressions come to me from Him: *"I am so very proud of you for all that you have done. You have put so much work and effort into this marriage and trying to heal from the betrayal of living with a pornography and sex addict. You have become something great; more than you were before. Now, take that new person and start today to learn more. If your life came crashing down today for the very first time, being the new person that you are, what would you do and how would you survive? How would you petition the Lord on your behalf, and how would you fight for your husband?"*

He directed me to a Facebook post. It was exactly what I needed to hear. It talked about faith. Trust and have faith that things will get better. Did I have enough faith to conquer these demons? Could I keep going and not give up? And on that day, I decided to fight. Fight for my life, for the broken pieces in my marriage, and for my husband who was being destroyed by addiction.

I sat in the car taking in the Spirit and the answers I was receiving, and I felt calm. My body gave up the fight and I let in the peace the Holy Ghost was offering me.

I then texted my husband: "Ummm, you may or may not need all new ties."

Yes! I actually cut all his neckties. Luckily one made it out unscathed that he could wear to church the next day, but all the rest had a two-inch slit cut right across the middle. He texted back with: "I know, I saw, and it's okay." I was grateful he was in a place that night to have that kind of reaction. It was a tender mercy that he could see my pain and understand my broken heart. And, wow, was it broken.

Only one other time in our marriage did I break something. We had been married about six months when I came home from work and found the TV stuck between stations on pornography. My heart sank. We had barely been married. I thought we were having the best time of our life. We talked about how we weren't struggling like others do their first year. We dated all the time and couldn't keep our hands off each other. We were totally in love. What did all this mean?

Over time I started freaking out. I couldn't stay at work at night. I cried a lot. I yelled and screamed. It was at this time that one night during a meltdown I pushed a ceramic bowl off the counter. It was now 20 years later, and here I was in full crazy mode.

I grew up with a dad that never disrespected women. Never did he tell an off-color joke, stare at other women, or comment on their body parts. I knew he was completely and totally faithful to my mom. It never crossed my mind that my husband would be any different. Back then, we sought help from our church bishop, and he gave my husband some things to follow, but really nothing more than live the gospel and try harder.

I now look back on that time at the beginning of marriage and realize I was suffering from something called *betrayal trauma*. I didn't know about addiction or the chaos that comes with it. Every day I'd come home paranoid that I would find something new. I felt like I was going crazy. We fought over trivial things and suddenly life became hard.

One thing that stayed the same through 20 years of betrayals is that I never fully trusted my husband. For 20 years I would question, check up on, ask and re-ask him if he'd been faithful. Not once did he ever come clean. He always had the same reply, "No, I'm good. I love you." And then lean in for a kiss.

Despite those reassurances, I never truly believed. I didn't know what to do. I didn't have evidence or facts. My hesitation was based solely on gut instinct. I couldn't put my finger on the problem.

In frustration I would yell, "There's something wrong! Something is missing! Tell me what it is!"

But nothing. There was never a moment of truth, not a single admission. I was left feeling uncertain now that my world was confusing and mixed up. Was it me? Was I thinking something was wrong when it wasn't? Was I paranoid? Or jealous? Or unstable?

No. I wasn't any of those things. I was right. Something *was* wrong. My intuition, my gut instinct, and my heart told me so. I knew, but I didn't know *what* I knew. That was the hard part. This world was new to me. I had no background to draw on and no education to tell me what I was dealing with.

I would not begin to fully understand until 17 years into our marriage on February 15, 2012. It was the day after Valentine's Day. In fact, Valentine's Day had been great. I delivered a beautiful, fun basket to his work filled with his favorite snacks. I remember thoughtfully picking out each item. I tied a big red tulle bow around the outside of the black basket and added a hanging silver heart. It turned out beautifully. I was proud to bring this into his work. I remember smiling as I placed it on his desk that morning. I drove over to the office early, before anyone got there, so it would be a surprise. It was a great day celebrating our love that ended with a romantic evening. There was no fighting or arguing, just our regular amount of good love.

At 5:30 p.m. the following day, my daughter and I stopped by his office on our way home. My daughter ran in, and I suddenly had a panicked feeling to chase behind her. Unfortunately, that feeling was familiar to me because of the underlying lack of trust from earlier betrayals. I was always on high alert, knowing I could potentially catch him in an act of betrayal. It was a fear I dreaded on a regular basis. This day was no different. I caught up to my daughter just as she grabbed the handle of his office door.

I started to say, "Wait, wait, wait," but she pulled it, and it was locked. At that very moment, that very second, I knew without a doubt what was going on. He was looking at pornography and masturbating. It was as clear as can be. And this time, I was not going to let him lie, manipulate, or talk his way out of it.

He opened the door with a look of shock on his face. I could feel the heat come up to my head. I stared at his eyes with a piercing glare and didn't look away. He tried to speak, and I said, "No, don't say anything. Not this time."

I left without another word. I was filled with pain, despair, panic, and disappointment. I asked myself, "What was my life anyway?" This confirmed once again that everything was a lie. He lies! My worst fear was true. My husband was a sex addict. I told myself I was not enough for him and that he needed something more than I could give him.

But the whispering of my inner voice immediately told me, *"No, that is not true. You have given him all of you. You trusted him with your life. You are enough. He is sick. He can't love you fully because he has a problem. A very big problem."*

Over the next few years, I would learn the true depths of his addiction. Knowing the truth has been so painful! I couldn't have ever imagined the double life he lived. Words cannot describe the pain and anguish.

I started seeing a counselor a year after this experience. He asked me to go to the deepest part of the hurt and explain what I felt.

I said, "It's...it's insurmountable heartache, grief, and pain from the depths of my soul."

He stopped me and said, "You just said insurmountable?"

I answered, "Yes, I did. The pain is so deep that it's unbearable."

He then said, "Well, what is it?"

I explained, "It's the heavy burden of betrayal. It's the feeling of not being valued as a woman and a wife. It's the fact that this addiction doesn't even let my husband value himself."

The night I found him locked in his office, I was in charge of a large church youth group activity. I was in such a fog. My head was spinning, and I could barely feel my feet on the ground. I just kept saying in my mind, "Get through this night and then you can think. Don't go there now. You can't. Once you start crying, the tears won't stop."

The activity that night gave me a time out from the shock of the betrayal. It was a gift from God that allowed me space to survive the blow I had just been dealt. I knew God was with me.

The time had come to wake up and deal with this. It was the beginning of a new reality. Nothing would ever be the same after that day. All I had known was gone. Over the next four years, I would be thrust into the world of addiction recovery and the parallel journey to find my own healing. Thankfully, I stayed in the journey, increasing my learning and growth through each step.

CHAPTER 2

Rise Above

You can rise above all this. This was the answer I received in a dream. It had been two-and-a-half years since that night in 2012 when my daughter and I discovered my husband's locked office door. At this point, we had been attending 12-step recovery groups, we found a new counselor certified in treating sex addiction, and my husband had completed a 90-day in-patient treatment program. We learned that we could only control our own personal healing and recovery, not each other's. It was hard. In fact, most days were hard.

Surprisingly, there were also beautiful, healing days. I recall days when we felt more in love than ever before. There is something about going through hell with someone and coming out on the other side. A deep connection forms through experiencing something so painful together. It binds you to one another.

However, it only becomes a foundation if you both want to heal together. During this recovery process, we had been in and out of this connection. It was pretty unsettling. One day it felt like we had arrived and then, within 24 hours, we were back to hell. I couldn't *make* my husband choose us. I couldn't force him to take his foot out of the other door. And at this point, I was not ready to walk away from him either. I was still fighting for us, for him, for me, for something. The unknown of what leaving could look like felt too scary. I clearly still had more to learn about how to actually submit all to God. I prayed for weeks about how to make it through the inconsistencies of my husband showing so much love one day and hate so quickly after.

After pouring out the feelings of my heart, realizing I had no way out, I received my answer. It came in a dream. I haven't had very many dreams. I wouldn't consider this my spiritual gift. But this is how Heavenly Father wanted to reach me at this time.

In this dream, the Savior had His arms outstretched. My husband was with me and I looked at him and said, "Take His hands." My husband took the Savior's hands. I told my husband all that I saw and wanted him to feel. I said to him, "Look at His hands that you are holding and how strong His arms are. Look at His face. He loves you so much. Look in His eyes. Can you feel it? Can you see His love?" My husband turned from me, then back to the Lord, and then back to me again. My husband had a joyous, calm, expression on his face, full of wonder. He said, "Oh, wow! I didn't realize that He loved me this much.

I didn't know that He is right here; wanting to help me each and every day. I didn't know I was worth this much." He kept repeating over and over, "I didn't know." It was extremely beautiful to see the light in my husband's eyes.

Throughout the dream, I joined the hand-holding and we formed a circle. But I wasn't supposed to stay. I kept moving back and letting him have this moment. I feel that it represented that I couldn't do this for him. It was between him and the Lord. And the Lord was ready and willing with each step he took. During this time, I observed from the side at eye level. But soon after, I viewed the scene from above my husband's head. I kept trying to get myself back to my original view. I had that feeling like when you're in water and you are trying to sink yourself down to the bottom of the pool but you float back up anyway. I couldn't stay down at his level.

I asked God, "Why am I above my husband's head? Why am I looking down and can only see the very top of his head, yet I can still see you out in front of me?"

His answer was clear: "You can rise above. You can rise above the pain, sadness, and destruction. The prayers in your heart have been heard."

Great things had happened and moments of clarity had come for both of us. But, despite my prayers, I was getting impatient. Now I wanted my husband to feel remorse, to learn something, and commit to practicing those lessons in the future. I wanted an apology for the previous actions.

Unfortunately, he wasn't capable of offering these to me at this time.

Addicts lead dishonest lives, and choosing honesty has been one of my husband's biggest challenges. When questioned about his actions, he has lied over and over, until at some point, after much prodding, he would finally admit the truth. It took my husband three years after stepping into our recovery journey to reply with a truthful answer from the first question posed. It was a huge milestone! Something to be celebrated! It happened one night when I confronted him and he immediately answered with the truth. At that moment, I was so happy and relieved. Finally! He finally is starting to understand accountability. It felt great.

The following morning, I started processing everything from the conversation the night before. I realized the previous morning was filled with manipulation and making me feel like my worries were wrong and invalid, when, in fact, I had been correct. I knew there was something not quite right. In fact, I always knew when something was off. And each time, he would try to make me feel like I was wrong and crazy.

I was happy that he finally told me something truthful, and then mad that he wouldn't apologize for the crazy-making blame-shifting that went on before his truthful admission. This is where my prayers came in. I not only wanted truth, but I also wanted restitution. However, in my dream, Heavenly Father told me I didn't need that yet. He reassured me it would come line upon line and inch by inch as he learns more and continues in recovery.

I was told I could rise above. This meant I could take each milestone and celebrate. I learned that one truth is enough in each moment. And that more truth will come in the future.

My fear has always been that if I didn't pressure my husband, he wouldn't choose recovery. What I have learned is that if he is living in recovery, he will gain all these things that I want for him on his own. He will get to a place of empathy and understanding. He will know that his actions affect others. He will feel the joy of the Savior's Atonement and understand the destruction of this addiction. Over time he will see—see himself, see me, and see the Lord. His life will be filled with mercy, love, and overflow with blessings. I knew all this could be his if he chose recovery.

The prophet Job lost all he had. One by one his precious belongings, family, status, and all he possessed were taken from him. He never cursed the Lord. I wish I could say that! I have been mad, really mad, quite a few times. And the Lord knew it. I yelled it at Him. I screamed it at Him. I cried it at Him. But after I finished giving Him all my thoughts and anger, He was still there. Right there beside me telling me He understood, waiting for me to ask for His help. Job was faithful. Though he had nothing left, he stood strong. And, after showing the Lord he would never forsake Him, the Lord blessed him with more blessings than he previously had. The Lord showered him with every blessing He could give him. Job stood up through the trials he was given and turned to God in his weakest and most trying times. The Lord, our God, did visit Job in his times of affliction. The Lord never leaves us. Sometimes we leave Him. He's never mad at us. He just waits for us to be ready and come back and ask.

This has been true for me as well. The first two years, I had so much pain. I would go to the Lord for help and answers. He would show me, but the pain was unbearable at times. I don't remember very many days where the swirling anxiety circle wasn't taking up all the extra room available in my diaphragm. I could hardly breathe. The buzzing from head to toe, that unsettling swirl of death, would accompany me every day.

As I learned to trust in the Lord and give the pain to Him, I would have days of freedom. The peace would come, and I would feel grateful for one more day of reprieve. It was the best blessing I could ever receive during those times.

Then that peaceful moment would be gone, the betrayal would set back in, and I'd have to remember to give it to the Lord once again. I had to continue day after day, hour by hour, and sometimes every five minutes on my knees asking to know how to let go and let God take the lead. Slowly, inch by inch, I began to understand. I had moments of clarity where I knew I had finally learned something I could hold on to. I've learned to recognize when "the crazy" is coming on and then I know I have a choice to make. I can drop to my knees and give it to God, or I can spend some time in it. To be honest, sometimes I want the pain. I want to make sure everyone knows how hard living with an addict is, and that I deserve better. I want to cry in my pity and be the victim. After a bit, I remember how pointless that is. I also begin to feel embarrassed and silly that I'm pouting. This is when I go back to the Lord. He reminds me what I have learned and how far I have come. He also reminds me that this agonizing trial has made me a new person, a much better person. In fact, it's made me a person that I love and admire.

I don't want to go back to who I was before. I feel stronger. I have endured hell, and I'm still standing. And not only standing, but learning how to thrive and have joy! I have *become more*. I can become the person Heavenly Father wants me to become so when I return to Him, I will be ready. I will have made it through and be filled with the mercy and grace of God.

Would I give up this trial? No way! I know that seems ridiculous. But, it's the truth! I am closer to my Heavenly Father and brother Jesus Christ than I have ever been. I know them now. I feel them with me every day. I no longer walk alone in an empty shell. I am filled with peace, hope, and love. Even when I don't want to stay one more day in this death trap of addiction, I'm able to stay because I turn my head to the Lord. He is my everything. I would be nothing without Him. He shows me how to trust Him. He guides me to know truth from lies, and He reminds me through the still small voice what I should do and say.

I recognize His hand in my life and let all my other self-will acts fall to the side. As I pray for this, He shows me how to surrender my will. I am strengthened knowing He walks beside me and is teaching me how I CAN rise above, even in terrible times.

CHAPTER 3

Hold My Heart

I'm just a girl. I'm just a girl who wants love. And there is nothing wrong with wanting my husband to show me and give me love. The problem is that my husband hasn't learned how to give that love consistently. For him, it's a scary kind of love. Sometimes he's present and totally connected emotionally. Other times, he takes my heart and steps on it. When that happens, I am torn up inside. My world once again breaks and I fall apart.

One evening, he made a disclosure about some things we hadn't previously discussed. He was reminiscing and "nostalgic" (using his word) about a time period in the past that was about twelve years before realizing the addiction. He had been working out of town for a period of eight months. He would leave each Monday morning and would come home on weekends. At this time, our four children ranged in age from 18 months to eight years old. While he was disclosing, he suddenly switched gears. His face and body language completely changed. He was remembering what a great time that was. He was totally living a life free from the responsibilities of parenting while hanging out with work people every day. I happened to know that during this time period he was also viewing pornography regularly. He paused for what seemed like minutes and I finally looked over at him. He was zoned out in a trance with a slight smile on his face.

I said, "It's not very kind of you to be talking about that time period as the greatest days of your life when your addiction was in full force. Let me tell you how those eight months were for me. They were hell. It was one of the saddest times in my life. Our marriage was falling apart and I didn't know why. You felt different to me. You were callous, rude, and unapologetic for your absence. I was also parenting our children on my own. I knew you had struggled through the years here and there with pornography, but I didn't know the extent or that it was an addiction. But I did know that something was wrong, very, very wrong. Each weekend you'd come home and I'd feel sick inside. I asked you week after week if something was wrong, if you had been viewing pornography, or anything else. You lied over and over again. And now you sit here remembering, with stars in your eyes, something that was built on lies and fantasy."

At that time during his travels I felt so torn. I knew something was wrong and I felt it was probably porn, but I didn't have any evidence. He was so good at making me feel like I was wrong. Deep down I knew, but I didn't know how to figure it out. I asked myself, "What if I was wrong? What if my instincts were off?" Things were already bad and I didn't want to make them worse by blaming him for things that maybe he wasn't even doing. How sad is that? I was taking on his addiction as my responsibility, believing I could fix it somehow, even though I didn't realize it was an addiction.

I cried a lot in those months and it was the first time that I really thought divorce was a possibility. During this time I felt so confused, so unloved, and so alone. Against my better judgment, I reached out to a past boyfriend for support. We emailed and talked over the next couple weeks. I was looking to fill a void of what was missing in my marriage. I didn't get what was happening to me. I was good at marriage. I was a happy strong wife. We had so much fun and so much love for each other. And now everything was spiraling into an unfamiliar place. I was searching for validation from someone else to tell me I was enough. During those weeks, I thought a lot about life, love, and the effects leaving my husband would have on my little family. I knew I needed to turn to God for answers. My inner spiritual voice spoke to my heart that looking in the wrong places would only lead to more heartache. I really had to dig deep to be able to see that regardless of what my husband was doing, I still needed to be accountable for my actions. Why did I want to get validation from someone else? Why did I think I needed that to survive? It felt like I was in survival mode at that moment. I wondered what was wrong in me that would bring me to this point. I didn't know yet, but I knew God knew and He would show me how to be okay if I let Him.

I apologized to this person for crossing that line of talking to him. I also confessed my mistake to my husband. My husband was so kind and forgiving. He didn't seem to care. He didn't even get mad or jealous. Nothing!

He just said, "It's okay. I understand. You loved him once and so it makes sense." But that wasn't really true. He had been acting out, lusting after others, and didn't own up to his own actions. He couldn't be angry with me when he was living his secret life. This was the perfect opportunity for him to come clean and be honest. But he chose not to. He let me believe I was the one having problems. Still, I gave him so much credit and love for being so understanding. I now see that this was part of the manipulation and deceit of addiction.

So here we were twelve years later, sitting on the bed while he is thinking how wonderful his life was during that most chaotic time for me. I was in awe. And not the good awe. I could not believe that he sat there reminiscing! I felt so sad. My heart broke again that night. After I described how those months were for me, he didn't really say much except for, "Yes, that makes sense."

I craved for him to understand how his words, actions, and inactions affect me.

I wished he would turn to me and say, "Oh my goodness! Of course those months were terrible! And yes, my actions were wrong. I'm so sorry I was insensitive about reminiscing about something in my addiction that clearly affected and hurt you, even though I had told myself at that time that what I do in private won't hurt anyone." All those things went through my mind as I lay there. But none of that happened. Not a single word, a rub on the shoulder, or anything that would acknowledge my pain.

The next day I had such a heavy heart. I was sad. He could see this but didn't say anything. I went about my day as normal. I wasn't depressed or laying in my bed. I got all my things done for the day. I just felt so burdened in my heart.

That night I calmly said, "I want to let you know I'm not angry right now, but my heart just hurts today." He got a bothered look on his face.

"I am looking for empathy and concern," I said. "I would hope that you would see my hurt and say, 'Hey, are you okay? You look sad. Is there anything I can do?' I'm looking for care."

He fired back with, "Sometimes I have empathy when you're sad or you cry, but I don't always. And I don't right now. It just makes me mad."

I replied "It makes you angry that I have tears falling from my eyes? I'm not yelling or getting crazy. I'm opening up and being vulnerable and asking you to love me."

He said, "Well, sorry, I don't feel those things right now."

I left the room. I asked myself, what am I doing? This is emotional abuse. Why am I staying with him? And why is Heavenly Father asking me to? Surely He doesn't want me with an abusive person that is so unkind to someone else's pain?

Over the next day I received my answer. *"You are still trusting in the arm of the flesh. Give your heart to the Savior. Imagine Him holding your heart. He will never let you down and He will always listen to your pain. He knows the plan for your life. And it's a perfect plan."*

Those words reassured me that He doesn't want me to be in endless misery with someone unable to change. But rather He wants me to follow Him so I can change and become who *I* was meant to be. So that plan meant I would stay married to my husband at this time. I also felt I still needed to be vulnerable with my husband. I still needed to give him the opportunity to hear my words and feelings while he worked on changing his behaviors. I needed to be true to me.

Sometimes he would be capable of coming to my aid and other times he would rip my heart out and stomp on it.

When that happened, and it continued to happen, I imagined the Savior holding my heart. That visual would get me through the tough times. I practiced that visualization over and over. Daily I would imagine my heart in the Savior's hands. It initially helped some, but not fully. But I kept doing it, kept imagining that picture in my mind and one day, it happened. I felt it.

It was nothing I had ever felt before. I was in my closet praying, pleading. I was calm and quiet as well as distraught. My husband did not care for me, did not comfort me, and did not want to fix what he had broken. He did this to me. He caused this trauma from the years of infidelity and betrayal. He knew what he was supposed to do. He had been taught. He had a counselor, he had been to rehab, and he attended 12-step groups for three years at this point. But, he would not do the work to gain empathy and remorse.

He went so far as to tell me he only liked me when I was whole and acting okay. I responded with, "That is an unfair comment. You cheated on me with so many people and you want me to just automatically be okay. You haven't tried to earn any trust back."

He said, "I know, but I don't want to. It's too hard."

I fired back, "You're dang right it's too hard, you big jerk!"

I didn't cause this. This is what brought me to my closet that day with feelings of heartbreak. This was the lowest point I felt as far as feeling empty. My love tank was completely dry and there was nobody to fill it. In prayer, I asked for the Savior to hold my heart. I expressed that I didn't know how to go on being so broken in my soul.

Finally, all my practice and obedience paid off. I felt my heart fill up to the very top and then start overflowing. I felt throughout my entire body what it means when the Savior holds your heart. It is a better feeling than any mortal person can give. It gave me renewed strength to keep going.

What I've learned is my husband doesn't want to be stupid. He doesn't even want to be a jerk. He wants to be filled with love, but he is learning and going through his own type of hell. The following day he went to his counseling appointment. He came back filled with love and let me know that he had discussed the situation and the counselor gave him homework to help him learn and change these behaviors. He recognized that he has a lot of issues to overcome. I appreciated that he was aware and willing to work on them.

As the week went by I noticed many changes in him. For the first time since finding out about his addiction, the thought penetrated my mind that his hell is actually *worse* than mine! I know! I said it! I can't believe that I did. Because my hell has been bad! But when it hit my mind, I knew it was true! That realization changed so many things for me.

All this time I wanted to help him. I wanted to help his recovery. I wanted to be in charge of what recovery should be for him. Because I knew that if he just followed what I said that he would be healed. Ha! That's the furthest from the truth. I thought I knew that if *he* changed *I* would be okay. I have learned that's not true either. I won't be okay if I don't allow myself to heal. I can only heal and recover from this betrayal and trauma with God. And my husband can only find his recovery through God.

I can't fix him and he can't fix me. I had been learning and applying this concept for a few months, but it was hard. Things were starting to sink in. If I couldn't control this addiction and his recovery, what could I do? I was starting to understand more. I knew what I had control of. And *this* would be the way to healing and recovery for myself. The way I had control of this was to *let him heal*. What does that mean? I influence his environment. Is it a safe place for a person with emotional problems and brain damage, caused by addiction, to become whole? If not, why? Am I creating chaos, anger, malice, resentment, and bitterness? I have done that, a lot of that. It hasn't worked yet. By owning my actions of how I respond, I have control of myself and my reactions. Now that I can see that his problems are way worse than mine, I can create a home of love where everyone in it can feel peace and want to become better. This doesn't mean accepting abusive behavior. This means to react with boundaries and keeping my feelings and emotions in check.

As I give my heart to the Lord while opening my heart to my husband, things can change. When I bring up something to talk about with him, I have to expect, depending on the day, that he will come back with an array of emotions. The good thing is no matter what the emotion is, he is feeling something! That is a step in the right direction.

I was told in a counseling session to think of things this way: he has a barrel. As emotional things come up, he digs down in the barrel. Because he is trying to change and live in recovery, he is at the bottom of the barrel. So, all he has to work with is what it's filled with. And the bottom of the barrel is filled with anger, guilt, and shame. That's what he has to work with. So he pulls it out and he's mad, angry or bothered at my emotions. And because I'm working my own recovery and healing, I can now see that this is GREAT! He is in there! He is no longer living on the surface, which is where he was when I told him about the communication with my old boyfriend. This is why his response was so unfeeling and numb. Feeling emotions is a scary and painful place for an addict to be who has never lived anywhere else except numbed out in denial.

As I give my heart to God to hold in His loving hands, I can give my husband the love and compassion he needs as he scrapes the bottom of the barrel to figure out his emotions. My husband loves me. And he tries to show me that love. But there are times when he cuts me down to the ground. I have new tools to use to conquer the pain. They are called "love and empathy." Empathy for him that I now know his pain is greater than mine. I have to pray multiple times a day to remember, but I can grant him a safe place to figure out his brain and what needs to be fixed. His feelings may rise and I will get more compassion and love than I could ever need. Hopefully, that will come from him. But if not, my road will be paved by God. And it will be a blessed road.

CHAPTER 4

Learning to Let Go

One night we went to watch our daughter's dance performance. We were outside around a small amphitheater and so close to the stage that the dancers were in our face. This is a teenage dance team. I knew I would have to use all the tools I've learned to keep from triggering, freaking, hyperventilating, blaming, and being angry at my husband. As we sat down I purposely sat with two of my children between me and my husband. If I was going to be able to do this, I needed space.

I took a few deep breaths and looked up toward heaven and said, "Heavenly Father, I'm so glad you've got this. I'm so glad this is between you and him. I don't need to take this on. I'm so glad I don't have to worry about how this is affecting him."

It was only about a 30-minute show but I had to call back to God probably five times. At one point, I said, "Now, remind me again of how you've got him?" Quickly within a second I was answered. The Spirit was with him reminding him of all he had learned to keep himself healthy. He had tools so he could watch his daughter without being distracted in fantasy by the other girls. Once again, I said, "I'm so glad you've got this. You know more how to help his mind than I do."

At one point I changed my morning prayer. In it I added that I no longer wanted to run any portion of my life. I want to say only what He would have me say, do what He would have me do, and be able to hold back my self-will and let it fall out of my life. Because I truly wanted that and couldn't handle controlling any of it anymore, my life began to change. For the first time in over two-and-a-half years I was learning to give it all to God and let go. I had always believed He knew more than me but I didn't know how to trust Him that He would take care of the daily tasks. But now, I knew that my way, my obsessing, and my tears needed to stop. I no longer wanted any of it. And because of my submitting to God, my life has completely changed.

What surprised me was how much I had grown and changed with what I had already learned. I didn't know I still had a ways to go. I didn't realize and couldn't comprehend how great this next chapter of learning would make me feel. As I have learned to trust only God, I feel the healing in my soul. If the healing could be measured, I'd say at that point I felt filled up to my knees, whereas before, I only felt healed on the outside. The feeling when the spirit warms you like a blanket, I had experienced that many times. I had also experienced times when my whole soul felt overwhelmed with the Spirit burning from within. But, that was only a moment. It wasn't lasting. Now the healing process was happening and was happening every day. I could physically feel myself getting better.

So, that day at the dance performance, I was able to prepare with God before I left. I knew it would be hard for me. I had been living in fear for so long since finding out about his addiction that I didn't know how to function normally in public anymore. I would start panicking seeing someone that I felt could trigger his addiction. What I hadn't learned prior is that anyone can trigger an addict. A person can be fully clothed wearing a turtleneck and an addict can make up a story objectifying that person and use them, like a drug, in their own head. But for me, I was in constant alert mode. Is he looking at her, or maybe her, or her? It was the result of betrayal and not having a trustworthy spouse. It was a huge breakthrough for me to let God take care of the dance performance. I didn't have to control any of it. I only had to stay present in my own mind with God's help. It was a turning point in my healing and recovery.

I continue to have beautiful experiences as I work on turning to God. But recently, I had a run-in with Satan. He was attacking and it was big. I recognized him and what he was doing. It took all the prayers, faith, and submitting to God I could muster to get away from him. He and his demons were trying with all their power to take me down. I was not going to let that happen. This brought on mental and physical pain. I thought my heart was going to stop. At one point, I was so exhausted from this fight that I lay down on my bed as I prayed. At that moment, I felt angels all around, and with hands on my head I could hear them say, *"We've got you, dear sister. You are protected. We are fighting with you and we will ride with you throughout the rest of this day. We've got you."* I felt as though the heavens opened and there was my dad with many others cheering, clapping, and excited as if giving high fives. They were cheering as if to say, *"She did it! She won the battle!"*

The adversary does not want me to tell my truths. He does not like that I'm conquering his lies. He is angry I will not give up and that I am doing all I can to fight for my personal healing and the repair of the destruction from this addiction.

During this time period my husband and I attended an out of town seminar put on by Maurice Harker called "Breaking the Chains." It was just what we needed. It talked about Satan's tricks and how he works. We both came away with new light and wisdom, hope for the future, and motivation to kick this to the curb. But as we got in the car to drive home I became overwhelmed with all that I still had to do. I also was very aware of where my husband was at that point. This was discouraging because I had to somehow make it through when I knew it was going to be a while before I got what I desired from him.

My eyes filled with tears and I began wondering how I could make it. And I wondered if I even wanted to? I wasn't sure I wanted to like my husband, let alone love him anymore. I had fought so hard for him and for us. He was not where I wanted, wished, or even expected him to be. I felt my heart becoming very sad. We changed places so he could sleep. I began to drive. I love driving. It's my time to connect with God and I knew I needed him badly to prevent me from spiraling. I began by telling my Heavenly Father how I was feeling. I then looked over at my sleeping husband and I said to God, "Tell me what you see in him? Tell me the good things and how I should see him?" The Holy Ghost whispered, *"All the stuff on the inside has to change before it will show on the outside. We are working on him and he is trying. He has changed so many things that you can't see. There are changes. Lots of them!"*

I was prompted to think of all the times I had been told over the years that I could rise above. I asked through a quick prayer to be reminded of the reasons and experiences I had been given in the past. Immediately, thoughts filled my mind:

It's okay to move forward.

He's improving inch by inch.

That day will come when he can be called honest.

He will continue to be more open and honest day by day.

He is trying.

He will be able to love you in the way that a husband should.

He knows he's not perfect. He doesn't think he is.

He is learning new ways, new ideas, and things he has never been shown.

These things flooded my mind bringing love and light to my soul. I started pondering on what a blessing letting go is and how I have really been learning how to listen and receive answers. It amazed me that the answers kept coming. They didn't stop until I stopped asking. I didn't want to stop driving that day. I kept asking Heavenly Father to help me keep a clear mind so I could hear and talk with Him. I wanted to know all I could.

He then reminded me of something I had learned from Maurice. We each had to build our own separate relationships with God. Then, if we both did that, we had a much better chance of meeting back together in a place of recovery and healing. In the past I had heard similar things but didn't know how to let go. What if I stopped worrying about him and he did nothing? What if he didn't choose God? What if he got lost along the way and never came back? My family was at stake. How was I to just let go? I didn't know how or what that meant. But it hit me hard during Maurice's seminar. There was no other way. In my mind I kept hearing, "There is no other way," and "What if he doesn't choose God?" But as I was reminded of that principle, this thought came into my mind. *"As you become your truth he will either drop out of your life and you will be okay with it, or he will want to be part of your life and come running behind to catch up before it's too late."*

I heard it and it resonated with me. I finally understood what he does or doesn't do has nothing to do with me. The only thing I had complete control of was my relationship with God. I asked, "How do I do that?" I heard, *"Fight the fight with him. Not against him. Wrap him in a cocoon of love and safety, guarding from self-loathing and shame. Create blankets of light which foster trust, padded from the out-of-control spiraling. Every time it hits something it bounces off like a cloud instead of a pile-up. This helps you and him."*

I think of the part in Willy Wonka where they drank the fizz and they lost gravity. They hit the sides of the tank but were never hurt. They just softly bounced. I would wrap him in a blanket of love so he could heal. As I have let God take over, I have been shown that I really have no idea what's going on in my husband's head. One thing may happen and I'll think how mean and rude he is. It is all I can do to hold back and not voice my opinion. By the next day, he's talking more and adding things to it. It's not at all what I thought. As I have prayed for the Spirit to guide him and show him his path, he has heard and followed. He has listened to that spiritual voice more than he has ever listened to me. If I can keep my light and stay in a soft place, it will not only help me keep my sanity, but it will allow God to teach and heal my husband. If I truly trust God, then I need not worry what the Lord is in charge of. I am so blind to God's plan. I cannot be in charge of it. Gratefully He can see.

That hour in the car was so beautiful. I had been burdened with doubt, sadness, and discontent. But now, just one hour later, I experienced peace beyond explanation. I heard, *"As you become one with God you will be so filled. Over filled! And you'll realize when you look over at your husband he hasn't changed anything. Yet you feel completely lifted and validated. That's God. He did that. He can do more than an earthly man can do for you."*

I looked over at my husband sleeping in the car and thought nothing changed in this hour, except I talked to God and He answered. I am healed of that pain. And my strength and love are abundant. I was filled with complete peace, light, and love for God, myself, and my husband. It was a huge change from the chaos I had felt just an hour before. This showed me how powerful it is to let God lead my life. This is hard. It's a lot of work to heal. The alternative is pain and never-ending sadness. I don't want to stay in this pain. I want to move through it. It was a testament to me that day that God could change me. He does it faster and better than I can alone. I know for a surety that if I had driven that hour talking to myself, I would have finished that drive sobbing and with no hope for the future. Instead, I was given a gift. And I took it.

CHAPTER 5

Daughter of a King

I feel impressed to talk openly about my experience toward finding God and coming to know Him.

In a meeting for my husband's church membership, I expressed my thoughts and feelings about my struggle throughout the years. I was asked to share the heartbreaking moments, the distrust, the lies, and how devastating this has been for me. I also shared my gratitude that because I chose to turn to God, I am no longer the same. As tears ran down my cheeks, the words came out of my mouth.

"Because God let me go through this craziness, and He has prompted me to keep going, I now know Him better than any other person I've ever known on this earth."

I had never before said these words. I did not know I felt this way until that very moment.

This was a shocking revelation to me! I immediately thought to myself, *"Really? I know Him more than I know myself, my spouse, my children, my siblings?"* Yes, it was true. I know Him now. I didn't know I could actually feel like I know Him as if we were best friends who talk every day. I didn't know that was even possible. I never thought that it is allowed or even attainable to know God and His Son on such a personal level.

God speaks only truth. He shares His thoughts, His love, and shows time and again His ability to be with us. I trust Him because He always tells me the truth. It feels easier to know someone that doesn't hide anything. We humans have so much going on in our thoughts; we can't possibly know the intricate details of our loved one's minds. I see that coming to know Him this much was a process. Over the years, I have learned to count on Him. I could feel His presence in my life. I heard answers to prayers and my testimony of the scriptures increase. I felt His comfort when I was flat on the floor in my closet as tears rolled down my face.

I know God and His Son. What I didn't know was that all the times I had cried or felt I couldn't go on one more day, and all the times I'd felt the pain of utter despair would bring me to the point of knowing them!

As I sat in that meeting with the bishopric, I felt the love of God so strongly and I knew that what I said was actually truth. The truth was spoken and reaffirmed by the Holy Spirit that I was not making this up. Our relationship with the Godhead can be ours. It will come in stages as we practice turning our face to the Lord, falling on our knees as much as we need to, and constantly giving our pain, grief, sadness, anger, resentment, and fears to God. As we do that, we feel Him and grow to trust Him. Trust doesn't just come. We allow those feelings by showing Him we will come to Him, even though we don't know what the heck we are doing. We come to Him with honesty and hope.

Sometimes I yell out, "I hate this!" or "This is too hard!" Sometimes I say, "I'm mad at you that this isn't going away." Or, "I had a good day yesterday, so why is today back to terrible?" I come honest and broken. And the realness of this pain and my need to be heard was the start of this relationship. Never once have I felt that God is upset with me when I'm mad, or when I cut my husband's ties, or even when I've told my husband I hate him so much. God knows how broken I am and the pain that is pressing on my heart. And He just loves me. He loves me exactly where I'm at now. He doesn't think I'm a terrible person because I can't get over it or can forgive only portions of the pain. He wants to offer solace and comfort. And if I talk it through with Him, instead of in my own head, then I'm inviting Him to share His thoughts on how I can make it through.

When I let the other voice in my head determine my feelings or outcome of a situation, it is never good. NEVER! Something else I learned at the "Breaking the Chains" workshop by Maurice Harker, was that the other voice, even though it sounds like mine, is NOT mine. Satan is very good at what he does. He can even sound like me. If that voice is negative and offering terrible, painful suggestions, I have to quickly recognize who I'm talking to. I don't want Satan running my life. *He's bad at it.* He makes everything worse!

Now, anytime I want to ponder or mull things over in my mind, I involve God. I open it up with a short prayer inviting God to talk. I'm not actually just praying. I'm conversing. But instead of talking to my crazy broken self about all the absurd things in my life, I talk them through with Heavenly Father. And when I do that, everything falls into place. I feel better instead of worse. I am no longer in a state of paranoia. And, even though I may not know the answer, I have a sense of peace. I feel heard.

This is a much better feeling than when I discuss things with myself. Discussing things solely with myself, without a doubt, leaves me in a state of distress. It puts me in fight or flight mode. When that happens, I've got the distress signal going off loudly throughout my body. I hate that feeling.

I need a calming influence and a quiet environment so I can think rationally. My trust can only be in God. It cannot be with the voices in my mind or listening to outsiders telling me what I should do. I only trust God. He speaks pure truth. His view isn't skewed like others in my life. Advice offered by friends and family, although they mean well, come from a place of their own belief system and life experiences. They cannot know what is right for you. They don't have that power to know.

With the endless opportunities I've been given to make the constant choice to turn to God instead of the world, I am blessed. The more I choose Him, the more the blessings stack up. Every time I give my all to my God, He pays me back with blessings. I have witnessed and experienced first-hand that after the hardest falls come the greatest blessings.

There have been times where I was certain there would not be another huge letdown. But I was wrong. And I fell harder and faster each time. As tempting as some of those times have been to give up on myself and listen to those voices that said, "*You can't do this, this is too hard, and Heavenly Father is requiring way too much from you,*" I held to the straight and narrow "iron rod of truth" with both arms. Even though I closed my eyes and dangled from below, I held on. I could feel my grip loosening. Those were the moments when my faith was tested. Who do I turn to? I felt so alone. I dug deep and turned to God in fervent and panicked prayer to save me. And as I proved over time that I would come to Him no matter how often this trial took me down, He blessed me to see more of Him. I chose Him. I saw Him. I chose Him again. He gave me more. And it kept going. The veil over my eyes, preventing me from physically seeing God, got thinner and it became easier to hear Him. That's how I came to know Him.

My deepest pain brought me to Him. Trusting in God and submitting my entire will has been the most amazing journey I've been on. He saves me from this pain and also from myself. I am His daughter. He is my King. He loves me and He loves you. He loves me when I'm happy and doing well and He loves me when I'm a complete disaster and unable to follow anything He is telling me. He has perfect patience, and, therefore, there is no need to punish myself incessantly for my mistakes. Turn to the Lord, naked before Him, and give Him your heart. Don't hide your faults or try to disguise them. He knows all of you. He's fine with your mistakes. Open up about them and see what He has to say about them. Even with your imperfections, He will show you your greatness.

Don't let the voice of Satan tell you your worth. Only God is capable of truth. So, stop asking your own head or other people. God is Love. God is all knowing. And God is the one who gave you life. That proves *you* are a daughter of a King. Your worth is great. Your soul is great. You are great! Let Him heal you. Let Him show you the path. Let Him show you that you can trust Him so the blessings He has for you can shower down upon you. The greatest things about trials are the blessings that come with them. And, when you come up for air, you will breathe easier knowing your life has purpose and these hard, terrible things are bringing you closer to Him.

CHAPTER 6

When Pain is Too Much

What do you do when the pain is too much? I'm sure you have experienced that many times. Sometimes I'm so overwhelmed that I question, "Why do I have to do this? Why is it taking so long? And why does it feel like I do all the work and have to make the hard choices? It is just too much." When this feeling of overwhelm hits hard, it takes me a few days to get fully out of it. I will go through moments of peace and clarity as I immerse myself in recovery and turn toward God. But the pain is so deep that the one moment doesn't sustain me. I've noticed lately that when this happens, I have to go back to Heavenly Father multiple times a day. This usually makes me mad. I feel like He's not hearing me or doesn't think I deserve continual peace. During one of these episodes, I was at the end of one of these experiences. I was up all night trying to work through what Maurice Harker calls a "Satanic Attack." I had given in to fear and was trying to get myself out. As I walked on the treadmill that following morning, I decided I would stay there until I understood what God was trying to teach. I ended up with 15 extra minutes added to my workout. I felt the need to change the wording of my prayer. Instead of praying that he would take away this pain, I asked him for extra strength to endure it. In my heart, I asked Him why I kept going back to this place of overwhelm the past 48 hours. I asked, "What do you want me to know?" Then I just waited, listened, and tried to hear.

While walking and waiting for my answer I was listening, through headphones, to some songs from a program called *"Especially for Youth."* The song "The Girl I Am" came on. The Spirit whispered everything I needed to know. If I didn't truly feel this pain and if He took it away too fast, I wouldn't feel Him take it. And if I couldn't recognize Him taking it, then I'd be back in this place again in a week. He needed me to feel the release.

I was swirling about the future. He reminded me that he had already discussed a plan with me a few days prior. I knew this plan was to start tonight. He had told me earlier in the week. He reminded me this morning that He had already given me the plan. I didn't need to rush through the plan and start fearing the future. He had already placed the step in-front of me. He had reminded me three times the day before that I couldn't start the plan early. And I had made it! I didn't ruin His timing up to that point. Yay for me! I had the exact words to use for that night. I was counseled to say nothing more than the plan. Then, in two days, the second part of the plan would take place. He had also already given me this second step. So I actually already had two steps in front of me planned out!

The fear of how my husband would react to this next step was paralyzing me. I quickly forgot that God was the one in control. He knows all. Not me. As I told Him how sad I was that I ruined two full days trying to obsess and control, and how sorry I am that I was mad at Him, He said *"This is how it was supposed to be. You needed this so you could truly see that I've got you and I'm guiding your every step."*

He really is amazing that He so easily forgives me of my imperfections. He is a loving father who comforts and loves His little child just as a righteous earthly father would do with a crying infant, whispering in my ear, *"It's okay. Shhhh. Be still. I've got you."* I had heard that from Jennece Kahuhu, who is an Emotional Facilitator. She works on the subconscious where trauma and other emotional stuff settles. As I was going through this conversation with God, Jennece's comment popped back into my head reassuring me that God does comfort, He does protect, and He is all-loving.

He asked me to put this song, "The Girl I Am," on repeat and listen throughout the day every time I forgot the plan. By 3:00 p.m. I had played it about 20 times and there were still eight hours of awake time left in the day. But you know what? He told me what I needed to hear. He knew that song would help me and keep my heart and mind on track. He gave me that blessing. And because He answered and I listened, I made it through another bout of craziness caused by addiction. I was full of peace and love, and I had no negative residual effects of the last two days and the mental struggle that occurred. Instead, I was filled with trust in God that He will continue to show me as I continue to look for Him. When I can't see Him or feel Him, I must keep calling and asking. When I have learned what He has to teach me, then will I see that He was with me the entire time holding me in His arms. He is there whispering sweet words of love and comfort to my weary soul.

With all of this, it's still difficult to do what I'm asked to do. That same night I needed to enforce a boundary. My boundary is speaking up when I see him not doing all that is asked of him by his counselor each week. This is tough for my husband. He has gotten lazy on his recovery plan. He is the king of re-writing what he thinks he should or should not have to do. It's painful to watch. When he's following the plan, he is on cloud nine. He loves meetings, counseling, and he is kind, loving, and happy. But when he slides, he becomes rude, defensive, blaming, and thinks this is too hard. This is the addictive behavior pattern starting up. I have to be strong and enforce my safety boundary. Each time this happens, I go into a nervous place questioning God and why do I have to do this. I ask, "Why am I the one that always has to have the hard conversations?" It's so stressful. Even though God told me what day to bring it up and gave me the exact words, there was still this apprehensive feeling. It feels unnerving to enforce a boundary. It has a racing feeling in my body, chest, and stomach area. It feels triggered with panic. It reminds me of when I have a trauma response and my legs are shaking involuntarily. But it's not really my legs. It's my upper body. There are no real words to explain this. You either have experienced this or you haven't. For me, it's a regular occurrence. I have a bit of panic when I know I have to do something that might have a bad response. I tend to swirl, imagining the possibilities of the outcome of this boundary enforcement. The great thing is that I do it! I still follow through. I have to. It is the right choice if I want to keep my peace and sanity.

God is directing this journey. If He says now is the time, then now is the time. He already knows the outcome. He knows why He's choosing today to be the day to enforce this boundary. He knows my heart and my husband's heart. He loves both of us. He wants to give both of us the best chance at recovery and healing. So, if I don't listen, then I am a big hindrance to His plan for finding peace. I'm back to controlling the situation again. And, seriously, I'm just not good at it. I used to think I was the best! I had everything planned out and was sure that if everyone would do things the way I wanted, everyone would get better. As I attended 12-step meetings with ARP (Addiction Recovery Program), did the steps for myself with S-Anon, and built my relationship with God, I learned that the only way to true healing and acceptance was to submit my entire will to God. It's been a long journey that is still in process. It's also been the most rewarding years of my life. To experience emotional death and then receive personal revelation from on high has been amazing.

Because I've experienced such opposite sides of the spectrum, I know the difference between good and evil. I know what pain versus joy, and despair versus peace, feel like. Because it has been so extreme, I know what side I want to live on. It's not even a question for me. I LOVE LIGHT! I see when there is darkness. I feel it in the room and I know Satan is there. I've seen him in action and I've felt him try to take me down. I can feel when someone in my family is in a bad place and I can feel the negative energy coming. Even if I'm asleep, I feel it and wake up before the person even gets to my door. It's because I now know Satan. I know when he has a hold on me or a loved one. And I don't like it!

Light on the other hand, is the exact opposite. It's beautiful and it feels good! It's an all-encompassing feeling of peace and gratitude.

There was this night early on after the first addiction discovery day. I was lying in bed and my husband was in full addiction mode and had gotten himself in a bad place spiritually. He started talking about all the things wrong with church views. This had happened two other times in the past and I had quickly shut him down saying, "I will not discuss this with you."

But this night I was so sad and so exhausted from all of this work I didn't say a word. As he talked, I stared up at the ceiling as tears fell down my cheeks. He just talked and talked. I was so heartbroken. Then the most amazing thing happened. I felt a definite division down the center of the bed. His half engulfed in complete darkness and my half completely light. It was so light I could see it in my mind—white and bright. Then I heard the whispering of the Spirit say, *"What you know IS right."*

My testimony was strong. I worked for it in high school and college, so I already knew for myself that the gospel of Jesus Christ was true. But that night I was weary. And listening to him talk through the darkness was almost more than I could bear at that moment. But when I was told, firmly surrounded in light, that what I know IS true and right, a smile came across my face. I was comforted in the arms of my God. Dark and light cannot exist in the same space, but they can be joined right at the meeting point. That night I experienced with spiritual eyes how real dark and light are. I am light. I *love light*. With all my experiences over the past few years, I continually get rid of things in my life that may not be bad, but don't add light. Going through this process on the roller coaster of recovery, I can't let any noise get in the way. I need peace. I desire experiences that bring calm and edifying results.

Writing and music are two new things I have found that have changed my life. I believe those things are currently saving me. They are part of my light. Music inspires me with God's goodness and reminds me I'm not alone and I can do hard things. Writing frees my mind and helps me work through issues, obstacles, and provides moments of clarity. I'm able to see more clearly and work through any insane feelings I may be having. This is also good for my marriage. I don't have to talk out the crazy thoughts in my head with my husband, who is unsafe when not fully engaging in recovery. If he were in a place of recovery then I would be able to share everything I'm thinking and going through. But while he is not in a healthy state of mind, I need a place to unload the chaos and pain to clear myself and feel grounded. When my mind and body fill up with stress I find peace as I write and it calms my soul.

I would encourage you to write even a few lines at night before going to bed. Or, when you have a traumatic experience, grab a paper and write out all your frustrations, sadness, and anger. You can throw the paper away after if you want. Writing will enable you to see the hand of God and bring peace to your soul as you get the negative feelings out of your mind. It will free up your spirit.

As far as that night's boundary, I prayed right before that I would only say the words God wanted me to say. I did really well! I calmly and lovingly let my husband know how I felt. He agreed and remembered that we had talked about what would happen if he didn't hold this boundary and keep me safe. I let him know I appreciated him not fighting me on it. I told him how much I loved him and that my main goal was finding true recovery and enjoying a lifetime together. This was not a punishment. I was being true to me and what God wants for me. Yes, it was hard. And my body was shaky. But after, I felt empowered. I had

God directing my every word. It went really well. It wasn't perfect. It didn't have to be because I was on God's errand.

Just a few minutes after, my husband's demeanor changed and I found him sulking on the couch. Luckily, I've also learned that I can't save him. He has to go to God in these times to find his truth and his healing. Who got you out of the pit when you were crying in your room on the carpet or sitting on the shower floor because you could no longer stand? Who came and picked you up when you were in your darkest despair? No one but God.

After discovery day, and the next discovery day, and the next, my husband didn't lay on the floor crying with me, telling me how remorseful and sorry he was. No. He was telling me to get over it. He asked, "Why are you still crying about this?" (I have to say he's come a long way since then. He's learned recovery tools and when he's living in recovery he is a kind, compassionate, and loving person.) But when he's not, and I'm curled in a ball on the closet floor because he verbally and emotionally kicked me while I was down, he's not the one rescuing me. So why did I feel the need to rescue him? It was a pattern we created for many years. It was what we were both used to. Through years of counseling, I've learned how not to try to be his rescuer. Now that I've been educated, when I see him sulking on the couch as if he's being picked on, I no longer save the day. I've realized what he needs. God has told me, *"Don't say anything. Don't do anything. He needs to feel. Feeling emotions are what will save him. Guilt about how he's living will save him."*

So when I see him sulking, I walk away. Not out of malice, but out of love. I imagine him in a dark pit. I'm yelling down to him to come up.

He's yelling, "I can't see. I can't see."

I yell, "Just look up. The light is right there."

Again he yells, "I can't see. Come get me."

"The rope is hanging right next to you," I exclaim. "Grab it and climb out."

"Where is it? I can't see it. It's not there," he says.

"It's right there," I yell back. "Just grab it. It's right in front of your face."

In the past, I would climb down the pit, place his hands on the rope and push his backside up as he made the climb. He'd get out, tell me how amazing I am, and how much he loved me, and that he's the luckiest guy to have someone like me in his life. Oh, how I would love that! I relished those words that I desperately wanted to hear. But dang, that cycle would come back fast and we'd be at the same place. Finally, through working my own recovery and learning to trust that God really would be there for him, I had to walk away from the pit. It goes back to the lessons I learned in my own pit of despair. No human person saved me. When I felt so alone I thought I could die, I turned to God and he showed me how to get out. He taught me where to see the light, how to grab the rope, and how to climb out myself with him by my side. Now, my husband gets to do the same. I still don't know if he will choose God in the long run. But being a part of his cycle was breaking me apart. I couldn't live another moment like that. I submit my will to God and I let Him do the work that only He can do. He loves my husband. It doesn't matter to Him that he's an addict. He loves him just as much as He loves me. God wants my husband to choose Him just like He wants me to choose Him. He wants him to be free from the addictive trap and experience joy.

I pray for my husband every day. I pray that he will choose God. I pray that he will thirst after recovery. Just as I have let go of things that don't add light to my life, I also have hope that as my husband continues on his path he will automatically let go of the things that hold him back. What a marvelous journey we are on. It's hard as hard can be. But as we look toward the light and walk the steps that our Heavenly Father shows us, we will be free and we will have peace and light in our life. With that knowledge, our pain does, in fact, become bearable. We can see who is holding our pain with us. We don't have to carry it alone.

CHAPTER 7

It's Better and It's Worse

Better and worse doesn't sound very good. It's the truth, though. As we find healing and recovery, things are so great! I am feeling normal. That is amazing. I did not think I would ever feel that way again. It is the highest of highs when that feeling of complete peace, joy, and love enters your soul. To have it stay around day after day reassures me that all the work is paying off. There really is light at the end of the tunnel. Even our intimate relationship changed. All of a sudden, we felt emotionally connected. And, for the first time in years, I felt completely loved by him. It was beautiful and surprising to both of us. He wanted us to be together without me crying, accusing, or being nervous. I longed for connection and love that hasn't been there for a lot of our marriage. We could finally feel the emotional healing. During this time, he watched a video of Dr. Doug Weiss teaching men how to help their wives heal through betrayal trauma. This video was the answer to my prayers. It hit him so hard and he finally got it! He understood the things I had been trying to tell him over the years. It hit him in such a way that he immediately put those lessons into practice and started telling other friends in his recovery groups about this video. It was such a blessing to see the light in his eyes for me and my healing. He now understood that he was the one who caused all of this. He was responsible for my trauma and what I was experiencing. This high lasted one week and five days. For 12 full days I felt on top of the world. We were healing. He was sober and in recovery, and we were truly happy.

Then something happened. I don't know what exactly. But he changed. And it was sudden. This kind of thing happens because he chooses to keep one foot in each door. Those twelve glorious days ended just like that.

I said, "What happened to you loving what Dr. Weiss said about taking responsibility for what you've done to me and our relationship?"

He was over it and no longer cared. This was familiar to me. I knew this reaction of back and forth. Saying one thing and doing another. I experienced with him many times over the years this wishy-washy, I-don't-care-anymore attitude. And it broke my soul. It had been three years at that point of emotional abuse inflicted on me by him and those previous 12 days were the best and most hopeful days I had felt this entire journey. I thought he was going to do it. I thought he was going to step fully into recovery work. It was so devastating that he didn't.

To mend my soul, I started listening to songs from the 2013 Especially for Youth album. "Even when your broken, He's going to love you, so pour out all your feelings inside." These song lyrics spoke peace to me. I listened to this album every day. It has the most amazing inspiring songs that always lift me and get my head where it needs to be. I needed this inspiration because the day had come to implement the rest of the boundary that Heavenly Father had asked me to do. I did it in just the way He asked. I scheduled an appointment with our counselor, Ryan Christiansen, to share the boundary with my husband. It was not a good session but I did what I had to do. I was asking for in-house separation. This means we would have separate bedrooms, bathrooms, and closets. This way he could work on his stuff and I could work on mine in our own personal safe space. My husband needed time to process things so I gave him the rest of the week to come to a decision that he could do this or he could leave the home.

When my husband finished rehab, we felt the prompting that we had one year to heal and see if he would choose recovery. We moved our family to a new town to limit as many distractions as possible to give us the best chance at surviving our marriage and family. It had been seven months since the move at this point and we were at an all-time low.

Sitting in counseling reading over my boundary letter I stated that we are right in the depths of our year of recovery. I read aloud to him,

"This year was supposed to be about us, and you keep changing the terms. Recovery, check in, what you do or don't do keeps getting rewritten. There were things you agreed to when I picked you up from the treatment center in order to come home with us. Those were non-negotiable boundaries. These were things you cannot change if you want to live with me. It is my right to be safe from your addiction. Still, you are constantly trying to manipulate the situation to work for you. The line doesn't change. The line is set. The fact that you don't stay on the line is not my fault. I will not take ownership of your emotional lashing out with rude comments and behaviors anymore. My boundary states that if you don't follow these steps you don't live in the house. So far this hasn't been kept. It's getting worse. I see it. I feel it and you are constantly covering your tracks. It feels the same as past behaviors. That feels unsafe for me. I set the terms because of what you did to me. It is not okay for me if you don't follow these rules. Your attitude and behavior toward me is too much. So with all the love in my heart and with extreme hope and faith that this is supposed to be our next step, we will be separating. I don't want you to leave our house. I want to be with you. It's called in-house therapeutic separation. My goal is still the same and that is to love you forever. I'd like it to be that you move out to the other room. You are not allowed at all into my bedroom. You can do your own recovery as little or as much as you choose. I'm also asking you to keep to yourself anything that has to do with placing blame on me like saying that all of this is my fault.

I still love you. I still want to be with you. I still plan on finishing out the year trying to make it through. This is the next step. We both need time to fix our own selves. I want you to find true recovery. But I can no longer fight for you to do the plan. Moving out will give you that chance to see if you really are doing this for yourself or only for me. This isn't a discussion. Boundaries weren't followed and now I need to protect myself. If you don't want to follow my boundary then you have that choice and you can move out. If you think you can do recovery better on your own I totally support you. My main concern is recovery. I would like us to keep what we originally decided and that is you will not make any rash decision today, but will take this week to stay in the other room. Think through the possibilities and consequences of what you decide. Think about your recovery and what will help not only you but our family as a whole. Then at the end of the week you can continue on in your new bedroom or you can talk to the kids and disclose to them your new plan of moving out to seek recovery. I hope that whatever you decide will result in us being together in the end.

That night after that counseling session we were very calm. We both felt full of love because the burden had been lifted. Even though it didn't go well during the session, that night we were okay. My husband asked to discuss how the separation would work. So I began telling him what I had shared earlier that day. Pride clouded his demeanor and he said, "I will not let you win!" *"Win?"* I thought. "Really? Who's winning?"

He went on. "I will not let you decide how this is going to go." He wanted access to be able to come and go as he pleased, in and out of my room. I went to Heavenly Father with it to make sure I was not being prideful in my thinking. God stated calmly, "I already gave you the plan. It's not your plan, or his plan. It's my plan."

Well, okay then! I had my clear answer. My husband could follow what I proposed or he could leave. It was that simple. When I had told him he could leave if he didn't want to follow the plan, he got fired up.

It reminded me of a time a year-and-a-half earlier when he was full in addiction but professing his innocence. Heavenly Father had told me that he needed to change some things or leave. He would not leave. He said I could take the kids and leave but he would not be the one leaving. He would make this hard on me.

The previous time, we sat with our kids in the family room and I let them know that I had given Dad until the end of the week to agree to some things and if he didn't, he would have to leave. I then let them know that Dad will not agree to leave so we will have to if it came to that. I wanted them to know this was a possibility. The kids cried and asked him why he wouldn't try. He was in complete denial. It was like watching a person I had never met before.

He flat out said, "No, I won't." He got up made himself pizza and came back chomping on it. My kids were looking at me like, "What is wrong with him?"

My son, who was nine at the time, said "Dad, just answer me this one thing. Why can't you just leave for a while like Mom has asked you since you are the one that caused hurt to her?"

He said, "Nope, I won't leave. You all can."

It was the strangest and most heartbreaking thing my kids had witnessed up to that point. They knew nothing until this moment that something was seriously wrong and their dad clearly had problems. The kids and I prayed that week that he would humble himself. By the next weekend, he had a complete change of heart, which was a massive miracle in our eyes.

So, now, as he was freaking out about this new separation, his words and demeanor felt and looked the exact same as the pizza incident. This time, I was ready emotionally, physically, and spiritually. I heard my answer from God and it was truth. I felt completely taken care of. If he wouldn't leave, we would. This time I felt good about it. We would be okay. I wasn't the least bit stressed over this outcome. I was prompted to not say anything more until the morning he was to come with his decision. He had a counseling appointment late afternoon and I told him he would need to let me know his decision when he came home. That morning I reiterated how it would need to be. I relayed my answer from Heavenly Father. I expressed my love for him and emphasized that my only goal was to reach recovery with our family intact, if possible. Heavenly Father had said that this is the easier of the hard plans. It's all going to be hard but this is the straight way to Him. He chose to stay and our new in-home separation began.

The following months were the worst. He checked out mentally, emotionally, and spiritually. That was really sad to watch. Gratefully, with opposition in all things, there was a good part! I discovered there was a way out if I wanted it. With God, we can find hope. Working my recovery and healing, I was able to feel the power of angels, of prayer, of tender mercies, receiving blessings, and witnessing miracles for me and my children. The power of God is real. There is only one place to turn to in those moments of despair if you want help getting out of your pit, and that's through God.

He knows all. He loves all. And He is the only one who can bring us out of the dark and into the light. It is hard at first to choose God, because it's not only once that we choose Him. We have to choose Him over and over again. He never said it would be easy to choose Him. It's the hardest thing we have to do. But the hardest things bring the greatest blessings. Choosing God means that sometimes we have to let go of people, places, and things. This is extremely difficult and tests our faith. Trusting God to bring us out of darkness means we have to give up all to Him and do whatever He asks of us. By doing that and giving our very will to God, we will find light. And that light will be more vibrant and full of love and peace than we have ever known.

Are you willing to walk blind, to take that step away from what you've always done or always known to find Him? To find yourself? You will only find your true self when you find your God. Then and only then, will you be found. Fighting addiction is hard. And watching a person you love fight with these two different people in their brain is frustrating and heartbreaking. The callous pizza chomping guy is the addict. He is not my husband when that guy shows up. But when his authentic self is at the forefront, life is really good.

I'm better because I have learned to see clearly when it's him for real and when it's his addict showing up. I'm better because setting boundaries makes me feel safe and protected from the addict. I've learned to stick up for me, choose me, heal me, and not let anyone abuse me. I'm better because doing these things make me feel at peace. It gives me freedom from the crazy-making effects of the addict. I fight through the bad times because Heavenly Father has asked me to keep going and keep working. This isn't a punishment, even though at times it feels that way. He wants me to become better. He wants my heart to heal. He knows that learning these tools will give me that peace. It's better and it's worse. And, for now, I'm okay with that.

CHAPTER 8

When to Stay or When to Go

The crazy thing about this is it hasn't stayed the same for me. When the fog settled after the first discovery day of finding his addiction I got the answer to stay. So I delved into 12-step recovery and prayed like crazy. I cried every day. I don't think there were many days that first year I didn't shed at least a few tears. It was hard. Not only hard, but HARD! You can't know what you're up against when you haven't experienced anything like it. Everything is new. I walked into my first 12-step spouse meeting with my heart pounding. Standing in front of that door, I felt like I had just sprinted up multiple flights of stairs. I remember looking at my husband as he walked toward the door for the addict group and I walked to the door for partners. I didn't want to go in, but I didn't want him to know that. If I let on that I didn't want to go in, I'm sure he would have grabbed my hand and run out the door. There was no way I was going back home with that man without knowing that he walked into that meeting. I needed hope. I needed something to show that God wasn't crazy for asking me to stay. We both went in and came out filled with gratitude. It was weird and awkward but I knew this was where we were supposed to be at that exact moment.

God told me to stay so I could learn and grow and so that my husband could start getting the help he needed. It's very hard to change or "get fixed" if we don't apply the things it takes to get there. Over that first year it seemed to get harder as each month passed. I was angry and had more hate and disgust toward him. Every time he walked toward me or in bed next to him, I felt anger, fear, resentment, and a whole lot of other emotions. Many times I would lie awake most of the night. I'd have to get up and go in my closet to pray. I slept there a lot. I felt safe in there. It was my own sanctuary of peace. I played inspiring music that uplifted and took care of my soul. I placed quotes on the wall and kept my special blanket in there for comfort—the blanket given to me by my sister a few years back. I received many answers in prayer in that closet and learned how much God and the Savior love me and want to show me the way.

In March 2013, one year after the first discovery day, I was in my closet pleading with God. "I've done all you've asked and things are getting worse. Something is wrong. He says he's clean and gets mad when I keep bringing it up, but something is not right. We've been going to 12-step meetings for 13 months now and our relationship is at its worst."

It was then that He said, *"He needs to leave. He is not telling you the truth. He is lying."*

It took me about three days to decide I could do this. I would pray then say, "Okay, I can tell him." I'd walk out of my closet, panic, and turn right back around and have to pray again! Finally, on a Friday, I knew I was ready. It was Easter weekend. And I happened to have my sister's family in town.

Saturday morning came and I said to my husband, "Something is wrong. You are not being honest and on Monday you will need to leave."

He freaked out saying all this crazy stuff like, "I'm going to make this hard on you. I'm not leaving; you can leave! I'm sober and you are crazy."

Watching this was like a weird movie. This was not my husband! He never said things like that to me!

I said, "I'm sorry but I do not believe you and you will leave on Monday."

That afternoon my sister's family left to run some errands and my husband left as well. I was freaking out praying in my head and grabbed some laundry from the closet. When I grabbed a pair of shorts off a shelf I flung them to the ground and a key fell out. At that moment, I knew it was my husband's office key that he had lost a month prior. I absolutely knew without a doubt, that key was the answer I needed. I was supposed to use it.

74

I grabbed it and drove to his office. I flipped on the computer, clicked on the history, and there, before my eyes, were sites he visited from the day before. Oh my gosh, I almost threw up. There listed in complete detail was site after site after site. Things I had no idea about. There were dating sites, cam models, Skype sessions, teen porn, and more. I died! I remember almost hyperventilating, saying over and over out loud. "Oh my gosh. Oh my gosh. Oh my gosh."

I thought we were in recovery! What about all the meetings we went too? We only missed a few that entire 13 months! My husband was a freak! He was a liar and a piece of crap. I was shaking head to toe. I immediately called my church bishop. He had been counseling us. He had been totally helpful and supportive. I told him all that I saw. I didn't know what to do. He said he'd call my husband that night to talk with him.

I then went home, took the phone outside, and called my in-laws. They knew something was wrong between us but did not know what it was. I would no longer keep his secret. I had tried to be supportive! I was being a good wife, letting him decide who should know because it is "*his* story" right? Not anymore! This was my story now! He was ruining our family! And I was done. His mom answered and they both got on the line. I told them about our entire marriage, from six months in until the present. I told them about February 15, 2012, when it all came out and we realized it was a full-blown addiction. I told them about meetings all year and then I filled them in on what I found that day. I told them I didn't know what I was going to do. I said, "He is a disaster. And I'm not sure what's going to happen. But you need to know." I finished and asked them to not call him. He didn't know I found all this stuff. The bishop was going to talk to him and then I planned to tell him that I spoke to his parents.

That night, life went on with an Easter egg hunt with my two sisters and their families at my parents' house. Nobody knew anything. I was in a complete panic fog. I wanted this day to be over. My husband still had no idea I had found his secret life.

That night we got in bed. He had a sheet of paper and said very calmly that he had a few things to talk to me about. I said, "Okay." I listened as he read off a list of everything that was wrong with me. He started with he's not a liar, he's sober and I better not call him a liar one more time. It went on to say how I was crazy, how I needed medication, and that my inspiration from the Spirit was wrong. The list went on with 11 complaints about me.

As he read, I studied his face and thought, "This is the saddest thing I have ever seen." Addiction is a destroyer and I wouldn't wish it on anyone. It had taken my husband who is the most wonderful loving kind person and turned him into a monster. It was surreal.

He finished and I replied with, "Okay, well I just have one thing to say." He calmly and politely said, "Okay." I pulled out my phone and read from the picture I had taken of his computer history. I went down the line reading word for word all the vulgar humiliating details. I read every single one. I finished with, "You will get help or you will leave." He began crying. We talked all night. He poured out his soul to me and apologized over and over. He then visited with the bishop the next day, which was Easter Sunday. Honestly, the bishop was such a blessing in our lives. We loved him. That day he should have been home with his family. But, there he was, mending our broken lives. I will be forever grateful to him. I realized how blessed I was being able to trust my church leader. I felt gratitude that at this stage I did have someone to go to that understood, at least, a portion of this ordeal. I have found that God doesn't leave us without someone to guide us. For me, that day, it was my church leader.

After meeting with the bishop, my husband came home committed to telling my parents the following night. As we sat on their couch, he sobbed telling them his story and how sorry he was for hurting their daughter. They cried for both of us. They love him so much. They didn't hate him. They offered compassion and love and my dad gave us both the most amazing priesthood blessings. In those blessings we both received the same feeling.

As we got in the car, my husband said, "I got the answer about if I should leave or if I should stay."

I said, "I did as well." We both said it and it was the same. He should stay. Sometimes the answer God gives us is right for today and wrong for tomorrow. It all depends on our willingness to listen and change and want the help required to heal and recover. I'm sure my husband would receive the same answer about me if I didn't want to heal and year after year was making our lives miserable because I was unwilling to use the Savior's Atonement for my comfort and peace. God would probably tell him that he had done all he could in his recovery and he deserved to be happy. God's plan is perfect for us and our daily situation. As we listen and are obedient, He will guide our every step. If I wouldn't have listened that Saturday morning and was too fearful to tell him he would be leaving, all that terrible goodness wouldn't have happened. I had to trust God that He knew more than me. I had to believe if He wanted me to have him go, He had a good reason. In reality, He wanted my husband to have an awakening. He was giving him the opportunity to be humble and seek recovery help from Him. It could have gone either way. He could have listened to me read that computer history and storm out. But he didn't. He made the choice to face his fears. God carried us. It always works best when I submit my will to God and follow His every step. He knows all. He loves all. And the more I trust Him the more blessings I will see in my life. Maybe not the blessings I would choose, but the ones that were meant for me.

That following October I was sitting in a class put on by the Togetherness Project and Maurice Harker was the presenter. Someone asked the question, "How do you know when it's time to leave?" I thought to myself, "How do you know when there's nothing more you can do? And how do you know when it's okay to move on?"

His simple answer struck me deep. It made sense to me. He said something similar to, "Think of your life as a tree. It's covered in leaves. Every time your spouse does something that goes against marriage and family a leaf falls off the tree. If he doesn't do the recovery work for himself but you continue to do yours, you will find healing and wake up one morning and that last leaf has fallen. You will just know. You are done and it will feel good and right."

In order to be able to hear God's requests, and more importantly follow them, I have to be ready. It is all about putting on enough armor from God. There can never be too much armor. Every morning I choose to put on my armor. It's my survival. It has become so innate that it is part of my morning routine. I can barely make it out of bed before it strikes. I immediately roll out of bed and get on my knees. Why? Because each morning I wake up with the thought, "I wonder what today will bring?" Hopefully as I get further in my healing I won't feel anxiety the minute I open my eyes. But for now, each day of my life, I live in wonder and I need to be proactive in making sure I'm armed and ready. One thing I have learned is to be prepared. I am striving for daily serenity. I'm working toward achieving happiness and peace no matter what is thrown at me. Guarding myself the moment I wake up is imperative. I cannot go a single minute without first speaking to Heavenly Father. He already knows what I will face that day. Who better to ask for what I may need! He's the one! He's the guy I can count on! This was never a strong practice before discovery day. I was pretty diligent at saying my evening prayer, but I was hit and miss in the morning. Although my bedtime prayer was sometimes on my knees, it was mostly in the comfort of my covers. So you can imagine that I probably got distracted, tired, and didn't spend the time I needed to actually pray the right way. When the world flipped me on my head, I started to pray in the middle of the day. I found myself suffering so badly that I hurried into my closet and prayed for peace and the clarity to know what to do. This became a regular habit. Praying many times throughout the day gave me new light. My bedtime prayers became very sincere and always on my knees. Still, I had a hard time remembering to start my day with prayer. I would wait until the stress or anxiety hit and then I would rush to the closet. I didn't realize what I was missing. I made a goal to start remembering. Sometimes I would remember as I was getting ready in the morning and stop to pray. Sometimes I would have already headed out for the day, so I would say a prayer somewhere in the parking lot. Eventually, I was getting the kids off to school and then praying. Now, my feet don't even hit the floor before I pray.

I have seen the blessings and miracles given to me as I start my day with God. As I said, I wake up with a bit of nervous anxiety. When I go to sleep each night, I talk with Heavenly Father and tell Him whatever is bothering me. We work through it and I feel peace. I have lost so many nights of sleep these past years because I didn't know how to give my emotions to Him. I didn't know I could. But, now I do. And my sleep is valuable. I handle life much better with sleep. After I've told Him everything, I am lifted. I feel totally at peace and whole. In my mind I think, "Awesome! I won't wake up anxious now that I've given this to Him." I feel great. But so far, since picking my husband up from rehab, moving to a new town, and my husband living in my home again, I wake up this way. I hate it. I really do. It's so hard to handle and understand. Heavenly Father is teaching me things about myself and I've come to learn what my core issues are and why I'm having trouble giving up control of the unknown. So to arm myself, I start with prayer.

Then I read scriptures. I have always read them at night. But now I do both. Let me share a story.

Close to 15 years ago I was struggling with feelings I couldn't get rid of from dealing with something from my past. These thoughts had been going on for almost 10 years at that point. I prayed, and worked, and fasted, and constantly had to be on guard with Satan trying to feed me lies about these feelings. They would not go away. Now, knowing I live with an addict, I can pinpoint when they were more prevalent. I noticed it was when things were not right in my marriage. At the time, I didn't know why things were off. My husband was off. Something was wrong. I just didn't know what it was. I took charge during those times and knew I could change it. I ordered self-help marriage tapes and workbooks. I tried all the tips of showing love and kindness every time I talked or he walked in the door from work. I was always searching for the missing piece. I thought I could fix it. I thought, "This is crazy! We love each other. What is the problem?"

During these times I would have to fight off past thoughts entering in my mind. One day I couldn't take it anymore. I got on my knees and pleaded with Heavenly Father. "Please tell me what to do. There's got to be something. I've been working on this for 10 years now. There's got to be something!"

Immediately in my mind I heard, *"Read your scriptures every day and this will be taken from you."* Okay! Wow! I got up, opened my scriptures, and read verses showing me God knows me and hears me. I heard, *"You will not feel the burdens which are put upon your back and you will be a testament that I do visit my people in their afflictions."* Unbelievable! That was the answer. So I started reading. All the thoughts went away.

After a couple weeks I slacked off. It only took three days of not reading and the feelings were back. I freaked out! Oh my goodness! I've got to read. So I did. Again, they went away. And again I slacked off and three days later the feelings returned. I understood what Heavenly Father was saying to me. Put on the armor through his word and you will be protected.

With that, my commitment to the scriptures was born. Oh, how I've gained a deep love for them! There is truth, love, guidance, and light in those words. I didn't know that. But Heavenly Father gave me the chance to find out. That trial of my faith was a stepping stone so that when I faced the challenges of today, I would know where to go for answers. By building up my armor, it has given me the strength to listen when Heavenly Father needs me to make a change. He is counting on me to hear Him so I can be healed and be an instrument through Him to my husband. Being guarded with spiritual strength has made it bearable to act on what is being asked of me.

I have been told an answer many times. I follow it. It gives my husband the chance to change course. When he does make a change, the original prompting also changes. When he doesn't heed Heavenly Father, the consequence comes. It's been a roller coaster of boundaries, consequences, fights, and a whole lot of love. I have been learning to surrender my need to know what's ahead. I have tried really hard to not control when he should stay or when he should go. I have given up making my own plans of what I should be doing. God is teaching me that through Him. He will tell me all that I need to know, everything I need to do, and, most importantly, when and how to do it. I will achieve this as I arm myself in His words and power.

CHAPTER 9

Peace through the Crazy Making

In-house separation was one of the greatest blessings during this time. There was safety in my soul knowing that I had my room to myself to process, pray, discern, and be grounded every time I wanted to have a conversation with my husband. First, let me say I love my husband. I want more than anything to find recovery and end up making it through this together. He really has great qualities aside from the addict mess. But because of repeated behavior issues, I am not ready to have him in my room. Hopefully, as he continues in recovery, he will address these problems. If not, the separation will continue and eventually lead to an out-of-the-house separation. None of this is easy. I've talked to many spouses. Some are working toward healing their relationship, which is so hard. I know because that's where I am. It's the hardest and most painful thing I have ever done. Sometimes I'm amazed I've survived. Some women I have met have spouses who didn't even want to try at all. They left their families and continued in their addiction and affairs. Other women I've spoken with could not imagine their lives living with an addict, regardless of whether they wanted recovery or not. Their husbands' actions were too deep and too hurtful. All of us are okay with whatever we decide. Heavenly Father knows that no two roads are the same. Our decisions and our hearts are individual. The personal plan for us is just that: our very own plan. We know in our hearts what we need to do. So, we do our best to make it through the trials of this excruciating challenge. With God by our sides, we can get through anything.

There may be friends and family that don't support your decisions. This doesn't matter. They are not you! This is not their road. It's yours. The fact that you are reading this means you are doing a great job—the best job you know how. Becoming educated about addiction, what it takes to heal, and learning from those who have gone before, is exactly what it takes to become whole again. I believe wholeness can be achieved. The first two years I thought over and over again that my life would never be the same. My relationship would never be great. The further in my healing that I have come, the more I believe this is not truth. I will be whole again. It is fact I will never be the same. That is true. But I don't want to be. I want to be new, different, and better. I want to have learned all I can from this, survive it, and shout to the universe, "I made it and I'm okay!"

I wish I could tell every woman who discovers her husband's secret life how much she is loved. And as she opens her eyes and heart, she will find a network of people to support her and show her the way. She is not alone. YOU are not alone. There are so many of us beautiful survivors that are awesome and are making it. The key is to take care of you. This is not about him. He made his choices. Those are his. It is not your job to coddle, nurture, and "support" him in his pain. Yes, support him in his recovery, but you can't fix his sadness and take it away from him. He wasn't thinking of you when he made those decisions that broke your heart. He's not sitting with you understanding the depth of despair he put on you. Nope. If he's in recovery, he is learning the tools to stay sober and he will do whatever it takes to find freedom from the trap of addiction. This is a long hard road.

For my husband, his pornography path started when he was 11. He's had 30-plus years being an addict. That is all his brain knows. He lies, manipulates, and turns everything around. He is the king of rationalizing and justification. He doesn't like to say, "I'm sorry." It has been a long road already and it will continue to be long as he works through each character weakness that he has associated with these behaviors.

It's important that an addict have a counselor if they want to see true recovery. I recommend someone who is certified in treating sex addiction. They are called CSAT counselors, short for Certified Sex Addiction Therapist. There are others that are good as well that may not have this certification. Just be sure that whomever you choose is not just a "make-you-feel-good, you're-doing-a-great-job," kind of therapist, but instead, one who works through workbooks, homework, and is helping to set a new life path for you. This goes for both the addict and the spouse.

With the help of 12-step meetings, church leaders, counselors, friends in recovery, and reading, healing is attainable. It takes work. It is way too easy to get caught in the spin cycle of trauma. It can happen in a moment. Learning to find peace when that moment hits is what you'll find in your own healing as you do the work. It helps to have the image in my mind of bombs going off everywhere. Fire and chaos all around, yet I am filled with peace and calmness in my being. I can walk through unharmed. This is difficult but doable. And when you experience your first moment of achieving this, you will feel a huge sense of delight. You will become empowered and in awe of how awesome you are! And you will want to share with all your recovery friends what you just did! Share it with me! I'm excited to hear your journey. We all celebrate together when our minds grasp something that we never thought possible but worked so hard to achieve. This has been one of the most rewarding things I've ever accomplished.

It's liberating to stand in front of my husband as he professes his innocence with clear conviction while *knowing* he is deceiving me and then having strength that very moment to calmly say, "Well, I heard what you said, but I don't believe you. I will know when I can believe your words. For now, I see your actions. They tell me a lot. I will see if your behavior matches what you are saying. I get a feeling of what energy you put out."

You know when you are in the presence of a person that makes you uncomfortable? That's what I look for. If I don't want to be around my husband or cringe if he tries to hug me, then I take that as a sign that something is not right. This doesn't mean that he's for sure acted out. It just means that whatever his mind is going through I don't feel good being around it. Therefore, I have a right as an individual to remove myself from his presence or to put up a boundary to keep me safe and my sanity intact. If I get a creepy vibe from him, I don't need to feel sorry about it and try to make him feel better about it. Even if it's my own insecurities and he is not at fault, I still have the right to take care of me.

Remember, he is the one who created massive chaos around you and you are trying to sort it all out. Be patient with yourself. Remind yourself and him that if you feel "off" toward him, that's just what it is. That's the damage that's been done. And you are doing your best to work through your own feelings. You have a right to feel however you need to feel. *He doesn't have the right to tell you that you can't feel a certain way.* These are feelings. They may not always be true, but they are how you feel, and that is true. The rest will sort itself out if you and your addict are each doing your own work.

It really is an ongoing process with lots of learning and lots of mistakes. When this all came out and continued to get worse over the years, my need for extra love and validation came out strong. I felt insecure, lost, and unloved. I got caught up in trying to control how he feels about me. This is one of my hardest issues. He has loved me before. I have felt real love from him in the past. We used to say all the time that nobody loves each other the way we do. We thought we were so lucky.

Well! That was thrown in my face when the second discovery day hit. The second time was far more traumatic than the first. When I went to his office and found the history of what he'd been doing, it was the worst pain I had felt up to that point. I thought we were in recovery, gosh darn it! He was going through the motions like a pro. And he appeared as if he was in recovery. So, when that happened my world fell apart. Since then there have been moments of feeling like that real love came back, but it didn't stay long. I can feel it from him when he is really working hard.

However, there was a time once again that I was told something wasn't right. Things were not good and everything about him felt off to me. One night we had a really great night and he offered to help me with something that I really didn't want to do by myself. He went above and beyond and showed real care in wanting to finish till the bitter end. Love filled my heart. My need for assurance came out. And I was thinking that maybe I would want to be intimate with him. Because I had felt so unsafe with him, I hadn't felt that for a while, so I thought about it and said to myself, "If he can tell me things he loves about me then I would feel good about being with him sexually." I told him what I was thinking and asked if he felt like he loved me in a positive way.

(I know I need to stop right here and just say "I know, right!" I was falling into a crazy cycle of... if this....then this.) This weakness of mine is not good. It doesn't serve me well. This feeling comes from a place of fear of not being enough mixed with the hope of being cared for the way I need. But I'll go on.

He said of course he loved me but didn't feel like he needed to tell me reasons why. I said, "Well, I need to know you love me. If this is even a possibility, then I want you to think about it and give me some things...even maybe a list." We got home from our event and he sat on the couch in front of a basketball game. I thought "Wow! What a total freak. I've offered sex, and all he has to do is tell me some things he loves about me. And he couldn't or didn't want to." This snapped me into awareness. I was starting to process what my sad part was in all of this and why I needed validation from him.

When it was time to go to bed, (he was still sleeping in the other room at that point), he walked by my door, I came out, and he tried to hold me and act like things were moving forward. I held my hand out and said, "What are you doing?"

He said, "I love you," and leaned in toward me.

I responded with, "You love me on the surface, but you don't love me from within. If you did you would be able to say nice things about me."

He stood there for a moment and said, "I really love you. I just don't have anything to say."

I said, "Yep. Goodnight," and I shut the door.

As I worked through what had happened with Heavenly Father, I was shown a lot about myself. One, for some reason, I'm still seeking validation from my husband. Two, I don't want a one-night stand. That's what it would have been. I would have experienced one night of some happy, but disconnected feelings. The next day he would have been back in his same place and left me feeling all of my same fears and insecurities. My heart would have been crushed and I would have felt used. Three, I absolutely shouldn't have to remind someone to love me. If he loved me in his whole being, I would know it and would not feel the need to ask.

Since then, I've been working on being emotionally self-reliant. I learned as I sat in my sacred church house that even though I *want* so badly for him to remember the love he had for me, he doesn't remember. He just doesn't. I know what he's missing. But he doesn't. I fall into the trap of being sad for us that he is going to let our marriage go. We will both move on with our lives and he will not remember the feelings he had for me as his wife. He used to feel so lucky I was his wife. I've often thought how sad I will be if he doesn't remember. But today, I saw light. If he doesn't do the work, then he won't remember. And if he doesn't do the work, I don't want to be with him anymore. So if that's the case, I will be okay. In fact, I will be great. I will know that this chapter is over and I will find happiness somewhere else within myself, with God, and maybe with a future relationship. He will go on living his life the way he wants and I will move forward, firm in my faith in Jesus Christ with the testimony I have gained as I've turned to the Lord with my whole heart. Christ has saved me from this hell. He has shown me light through the darkness and given me a path to follow. I know for certain that if I stay with God, it's a much safer and saner path then if I put my trust in my husband. I have felt uncertainty again as the Spirit has testified multiple times this past month to not trust my husband because he is not being honest. I know this. I believe it. I can see it. Addiction cannot be controlled as that cycle of behavior just comes back around over and over again. It will keep coming as long as the addict doesn't change his patterns.

One night my husband tried to turn it all around and tried to convince me of his innocence. I left that conversation unsettled. I know the Spirit had told me truth. My husband then sat and told me his own truth and was mad I didn't believe him. I'm sure you can see and have felt in your own life this crazy-making dilemma. The only place to take this is to God in prayer. He reminded me with firmness in my heart and unwavering conviction that He had already spoken to me. He had given me the safety plan of in-house separation which was in force and needed to stay that way. This showed me that addicts can't be trusted and that I should listen to God. If God still wanted me to keep up the separation, then my nervous gut feelings were right. I needed to trust myself and His plan for me by dismissing the words spoken from the addict person inside my husband.

I love Heavenly Father so much. He did not reprimand me that I came back unsure, asking for a reminder of what He told me. He reminded me of His love and that He was watching over me. I am grateful that He lets me know what I need to know when I need to know it. I can find comfort in those moments when I don't know why my husband is not transparent and I don't know the details of what is going on. I have to stay with God so I don't get caught up in the unknown. I repeat in my mind, "What is it I know? What are the truths I know?" I begin by going through each thing I can think of. Doing this brings me extreme peace remembering what is solid truth. I find hope and healing in that knowledge. The things I firmly know come from God. The unknowns, the insecurities, and the scary "what ifs" all come from Satan. He is not who I follow. In fact, as I have felt him trying to persuade me, I have calmly told him I know who he is and that he's not tricking me. I'm not falling for his tactics and lies. I notice how he's trying to get around me with different angles, but I'm not going to fall for it. I see him. I know who he is. He can't get to me so he needs to leave. I once again draw on the truth and knowledge from the healing God has so mercifully granted me while I keep moving forward on my path. I sometimes fall into my own traps of behaviors, but I am becoming more aware of them. In those times, I realize that I am not listening to my own inner spirit. By recognizing this, I can get back on the path quickly. Just like that night when I was pleading for my husband and he couldn't give it. The awareness of my own weakness rushed into my head and my heart. It only took me an hour to see what I had done and how I wasn't being true to my own spirit and my worth as a beautiful daughter of God. I did cry a bit that night in the sadness of missing that intimate piece found in a relationship, but it was only for a few moments. Even though I missed it, Heavenly Father was right there. He whispered kindly and sweetly that I am loved by Him and there is no greater love that can be had. I just needed to continually accept it and take it into my soul. Since then, I have felt complete. It's true I don't need my husband to tell me anything. Would it be nice? Of course! Would it be ideal? In my mind, yes. But luckily, I'm just along for the ride. As I look for the signs to follow and I heed the direction given, I will continue to grow and learn in this ongoing process. And, gratefully, after these years of healing, I love the ride more often than not. And that is something to be joyful about.

CHAPTER 10

How Did I Survive?

I think of the many days and hours I spent on my closet floor. Sometimes I was crying so hard that my eyes were almost swollen shut while lying on my back. My arms were outstretched looking toward heaven in the middle of the night because I could not breathe sleeping next to my husband. I brought my pillow and blanket in with me knowing I would be there for a while. I spent hours laying there with Mormon Tabernacle Choir music on repeat as it spoke softly to my wounded soul. I was broken. The damage had been done and every time I thought there might be some progress, new things came to light and I'd be hit by the betrayal truck all over again. Looking into my husband's eyes as he told me lie after lie was sometimes more than I could bear. I poured my heart out to God in tears of frustration and sadness. Sometimes I was so angry I didn't know what to do. I pleaded with God to show me how.

There were times when I didn't want to do this anymore. I just couldn't do this for another day. There was even one time as I sat in my closet that I no longer wanted to live. This was new for me! In 40 years I had never thought of suicide. On this particular day, it became real. I remembered pain pills that were in my medicine cabinet from my daughter's surgery. I said to myself, "I could just take them." It was too painful to handle anymore. I didn't know what I was doing or how to make sense of this.

Addiction is nuts! It is unmanageable. It has a mind of its own. It can't be controlled. His addiction and all the betrayal from his choices brought me the saddest and most chaotic pain I had ever experienced. It had been two years of torment and I saw no changes. In fact, things were getting worse and I didn't know why. I'd soon realize that my husband's addiction had spiraled and he had hit rock bottom. But sitting in my closet that day, I didn't know this. All I knew was I was trying everything I could possibly do while my life was spinning out of control. The verbal and emotional abuse was in full swing. I endured countless looks of disgust showing his disapproval that I wasn't getting over this. The laughing and mocking at my tears cut the deepest scars.

I have not suffered from depression before or ever had thoughts of suicide, but on this day, it was a very real feeling. A month prior, I had been prompted to throw out pills that I had from a past surgery with the thought that I had lots of teenagers in my home. I knew that prescription drugs were a problem in the high school. I didn't want any kids stealing them from my house. I hadn't thrown them away. That prompting was really a safety measure for me. I didn't see that before. How could I? I hadn't felt suicidal before. I didn't listen. I didn't throw them out when I was asked.

On that day, the memory of those pills came up. The thought entered my mind that I had them and could use them if I wanted to end this turmoil. I was still thinking clearly enough to recognize this influence *as Satan* and I immediately went to my knees in prayer. It was a fast and furious prayer, almost in a bit of panic. I was afraid of my thoughts and scared of myself at that moment. I was prompted to flush those pills down the toilet. I heard the prompting. I understood the prompting. But I also had Satan sitting right there telling me that I had gone through so much already. I sat with this battle for two days. I never took them out of the cupboard. I never looked at them. I just knew they were there. The Holy Spirit reminded me several times that now would be a good time to get rid of them. Each time I would say, "I'm not ready." At this point, I no longer wanted to take my life. However, the idea that I had control of ending the madness prevented me from doing what I needed to do.

It took me two days to do it. When I finally threw them away, the hold Satan had on me completely disappeared. Experiencing those thoughts was a frightening feeling. I love and reach out in my heart to those of you that suffer this battle. God knows how hard you try. He wants to help you. I can't begin to know what you need or the struggle you face. I plead with you to seek out the help and the support necessary to get you through. On that day I was rescued as I let the feelings from the Holy Ghost win over the feelings of the adversary.

God is always right. When feelings of fear, hate, anger, or frustration surface, it comes from Satan. When it is from God, it comes from a place of love, peace, and comfort. As I continued to recognize God, I learned to trust and follow Him. This kept me in a safe place of healing and recovery.

Survival in this journey is not just staying alive physically. It's about mind, heart, and spirit. Feeding those areas in us will help us survive and heal. Each of those areas needs to be nurtured in specific ways. My mind needed education. I didn't understand addiction at all. My mind told me I wasn't enough and that somehow it was my job to make sure my husband was not acting out in his addiction. My mind believed that I should be fixing him. If I couldn't, then I was flawed in some way.

I learned to change my mind's way of thinking by reading addiction-related books, meeting with my counselor, discussing healthy patterns of thinking, and working the 12 steps of recovery. My heart was emotionally broken into pieces. I fed my heart by regularly seeing my counselor, working with my emotional facilitator, and by talking openly with safe people about how I felt. Finding safe people is important. Building a support team will fill you up with love and will stabilize the unsteady and uncertain future. My spirit needed to be edified with faith, hope, and light. I needed more prayer. I listened as I was prompted to add in new things spiritually. My church temple became a regular place for me to go visit and my church's 12-step recovery group brought the Spirit so strongly. Imagine a very inspiring faith-based testimony meeting. Increase that ten times and that's the spirit that is in those weekly meetings.

It takes a team. I believe Heavenly Father has put our personal team in our path for us to find. We need to dig deep and find our inner strength to search out who is on our team. I have found my team in church leaders, counselors, and 12-step addiction recovery groups. These groups are where I found my closest friends. I love them so much. We joke how we know each other's deepest darkest painful truths, yet we don't even know each other's favorite color!

I couldn't have done this alone. I wouldn't have survived this process alone. I needed people. I needed to know I wasn't the only one going through this. I learned that my situation and story were echoed among many others. As I have met hundreds of women struggling with the effects of their spouse's addiction, I am in awe of God's goodness in showing me that this trial is not unique to my life.

It's not only me who is suffering. If it was, I can see how it might play out in my head. "I must be the worst wife, the ugliest, stupidest, non-talented, most pathetic woman out there. My husband is doing these things because I am dumb and not enough." It may feel that way at first when your world is turned upside down and you think you are the only one in the history of the world who is going through this hell.

How reassuring it is to find countless women with your same hurt. None of us would wish this upon any other woman. It is overwhelming to deal with so much struggle. There is the constant burden of deciding to stay or go, to try harder or give up. But when we find someone with similar experiences and we see our pain in their eyes, we connect. We want to immediately reach out and hug that person. We know that they know! And that is God's gift. He doesn't let this happen to us. The agency of our loved one dragged us into this. God does not control people and their choices. But He does stand by us, lift us, carry us, and hold us. He carries us and drops us in front of people who can suffer with us, hug us, and tell us they understand. The blessing through this trial is God's gift of people who understand and can relate. He gave us the Savior, who hears our cries in the middle of the night when we just can't handle another second. The Savior can help us with everything. God also knows that we are earthly beings who need to reach out to people on earth in a tangible way.

I came home from a group meeting one night and was reflecting on the greatness of women. Even in our saddest moments, women reach out to help another sister in need. I witnessed this as I talked with four other ladies at the end of the meeting. We stood in the parking lot for close to an hour discussing our needs and offering support to one another.

One young girl, probably in her early twenties, felt so sad. She talked about how she doesn't usually take the heartache of addiction personally, but today it felt personal. Tears fell from her eyes and I could feel her pain. As she spoke through her pain, we listened intently with empathy and love. She also expressed her testimony and love for the Savior. She testified that He is there for us every time we come to Him. She cried as she testified of truth and light. I saw how she was reminded once again of how much she is loved.

Earlier that evening, I had no idea this young woman was suffering. She offered help during the meeting and shared her knowledge. She had told me and the others that we are not alone. Then, to find out later that she was hurting as well showed me that God doesn't want us to do this by ourselves. We can help each other. Even in the midst of our own heartbreak, we still have the desire to help our fellow sufferers, just as this girl did that night.

We genuinely want to show our understanding because we know how it feels to be married to an addict. It hurts. It hurts terribly! Knowing that we all understand what this pain feels like is comforting. None of us wants others to experience this heartache, but since we all are going through it, we might as well do it together. Hearing other women share their stories, bare their burdens out loud, and testify of the things they have learned, lifts us. I have become more because I've learned from them. They taught me new things, different ways to see, showed me how to move forward, and how to set boundaries.

Honestly, it took me two years to understand what a boundary even was. Once that idea finally connected in my brain, I have been better! I understand now what it means to detach with love and to set limits. I am able to love myself enough to keep myself safe and protected. I could not wrap my head around that concept when I first heard it. As I've continued to do the work in counseling and attend my group meetings, God has blessed my brain with clarity and understanding. And when the idea of boundaries finally made sense, healing *me* finally started coming together. I could visualize surviving and having joy again in my life. It was attainable. I would have it. Eventually I would be okay and my life would be great. I just needed to use all the resources Heavenly Father had provided for me to learn, grow, and heal.

CHAPTER 11

Loving My Addict

Sometimes it is hard, almost impossible, to love my addict. The pain and hurt are all so real. Sometimes those fears take over. Well, I'll be honest. In the first couple of years, fear ALWAYS took over. I lived in fear of the unknown, the what ifs, the future, and if recovery was even possible. But as I've progressed, I've received the right kind of help, met the right people, and worked on my healing. There are now more days living in love than in fear. I didn't say "being in love." I said "living in love." Being in love is a sort of blissful floating feeling of intense happiness and joy. The love I speak of is more than that. In fact, most of the time it doesn't even include blissful feelings. Living in love feels like being grounded to the earth, feet firmly on the ground, with my head straight ahead, and a mission in mind.

My mission is to find out who I really am, how to become her, and how to love deeply. I show love to my husband whether he does as I wish or not. I'm still actively working on this. This is a new concept for me as I've struggled in the past to understand detaching with love. I didn't quite know how to process this thought. Detaching felt mean, as if I didn't want to try anymore. It felt like a bad thing. I realized I just didn't understand the meaning. My brain had a block toward the word "detach" to mean anything positive. As I've opened my heart and eyes to the Spirit, I am learning that I can detach. I can still feel love for my husband, and have joy, especially when I detach. Because my husband was living in the guest room and is not invited into our room, I was able to practice detaching with love. The day he moved his stuff out, I felt an extreme amount of love for him. I felt grateful that he chose to honor my boundary. I was at peace with Heavenly Father's plan for us.

I have enjoyed knowing I can just be myself in my room. I can read when I want, pray when I want, cry when I need to, and just breathe. This has given me the opportunity to work on my feelings with Heavenly Father when they arise. When I feel threatened by future possibilities, I go immediately to the Lord. When I feel that knot of loneliness or despair trying to creep in, I go to the Lord. He quickly sets me straight and I'm on my way.

Developing deep love is going to take time. I don't want to feel it out of obligation or to prove I can do this. I desire to feel the same feelings the Savior has for my husband. If I can learn this, then the sadness and blame of my husband ruining my life will completely disappear. I know this because on the days when the Spirit speaks love and empathy to my heart, all ill feelings toward my husband go away. They fully leave my soul and I have nothing left but a peaceful and grateful loving heart. With each night we spend apart, I am working with Heavenly Father to learn how to have complete love, to feel deep love, and to be shown what that means to me. I also want to be shown what my husband needs from me.

Why am I doing this? Why am I trying so hard to figure this out? It's because at that point I had chosen stay. I had a full disclosure of his addiction and it was terrible and painful. But I am here trying to make it work. God is showing me the path. He loves me so much. I know this because He has told me many times. He has told me because I have practiced going to Him in my time of need. With every prayer and act of obedience I get to know Him more and the veil between us is lifted. I feel Him around me because He is there.

Someone in my 12-step group once said "I love that I feel like I'm Heavenly Father's favorite child." This startled me. I never thought of it this way. But I had thought many times before that I felt so close to Him knowing He loved me so much. I've felt like His favorite before. I have even asked if He talks to others and gives blessings to others like He has to me. Well, of course He has! He wants to give them to all of us. He does give them to all of us. We just sometimes take a while to ask Him. And, sometimes we choose not to see. But that night, after I heard the words that someone else felt like she was His favorite, it went deep into my soul. I knew this was true for me.

My sisters, my sister-in-law, and I joke that each of us felt like Dad's favorite. He passed away suddenly in March 2014. At his funeral, my sister-in-law said in her talk that she gave that she was my Dad's favorite. We laughed. But you know what? It was true! My Dad loved everyone. Everyone he met felt like they were important to him. He was the best example of living in love. That is how Heavenly Father feels about each of us. He loves us all the most. Knowing that is so amazing. He has the power to love all. We are all His children.

I don't love any of my children more than another. I love them for their differences. I love them when they are happy, and I still love them when they are struggling. In fact, my heart aches for them in a way that only a parent can feel when they are going through hard times. So when I look at it like that, I understand that Heavenly Father aches for my husband to find help. He loves unconditionally no matter the choices he makes. He loves him as much as He loves me. I would guess that He feels even a bit more love when my husband is struggling. With that knowledge, I want to develop this kind of love.

When my husband is not demonstrating recovery behaviors, I have a tendency to go immediately to hate, disgust, and fear. Usually I express it to him with an ugly tone and mean look on my face. That's not good! That's not even kind of okay. That's emotional abuse on my end.

I would justify my behavior with, "But he's probably going to lie and hurt me again. He's probably already relapsed and I don't even know it. Forget it. I'm done with him. He's an idiot and he can't see what he's giving up."

When I do this, I'm in the wrong! I'm the one mixed up! I don't actually *know* any of those things running through my head. It's a made-up story that spirals me into fear. Just like I'm on my roller coaster of emotions through my healing, he should get to be on his roller coaster of recovery. I want to be able to work through my pain, yet I don't like him working through his? I expect total recovery from him right now with no more pain added to my heart. The pain scares me. The thought of having more trauma causes me to panic. But that is completely unreasonable to expect that from him.

What I do feel okay about is setting my boundaries for safety and sticking to them. He can live a life in recovery and be with us, or he can move on with his life on his own. That is all true and all okay. Instead of freaking out when his behavior doesn't look like recovery, I read through my boundaries and put one in place. Then I feel safe and he can make his choice of acceptance or consequence. Doing this keeps me in that calm place of peace and being detached with love.

I have come to the point where I don't feel my love is connected to his recovery. I love him regardless. I may not choose to stay with him, but that won't be because of a lack of love. That will be because of my need for safety. I feel better in this place. I'm not so tied to what he is or is not doing. I haven't been experiencing extreme highs of love and then hate as I have in the past. I am able to stay a bit more even. This is creating a calm state of peace for me. How I wish I could have learned that early on! But that's not how this works. Our journey takes us through each piece, one at a time. I'm here now, filled with hope and healing for my future. I feel so good with the things I've learned and what Heavenly Father is teaching me.

I was so focused on wanting my husband to know how I feel, and wanting so much for him to understand my pain, that I rarely looked at him and his pain. Now, I'm trying to get outside myself. I no longer pray that he will know what he put me through. I no longer ask Heavenly Father to help him understand. Instead I now ask for Him to show me how my husband feels, what his pain is, and how I can be of help to him. If I truly am honest with wanting to love him the way the Savior loves him, then I will want to put my selfish desires of love and true intimacy aside and get to know my husband and the spirit within him that is so desperately lost. This is what I believe is "living in love"— to forget myself and think of him. Why did he turn to pornography? What turmoil has it caused in his own soul throughout all these years? What does his heart feel deep within, behind the excuses and the facade of ignorance? How does he need to be cared for during the hardest days of his life? This way of thinking does not mean I am forgetting myself. This means I have done so much work in my healing that I finally can see there is someone else that is also hurting.

The hardest part is loving him silently. My husband, and I'm sure many of yours, lives only on the surface. They will shun, lie, or bully you into thinking you are crazy and stupid. They will argue that they don't have any underlying feelings on a deeper level. They don't know how to feel them or access them until they work with a counselor to remove the layers. We are spiritual beings who came from Heaven. We are children of a loving Heavenly Father. We all feel sad and hurt by our actions. We know deep in our spirits the damage that is being done. We may not be able to accept truth at first, but as we keep working and keep trusting in God and the process, we will break down our walls and be able to see what has been hidden for so long.

I did not see clearly for two years the damage I was doing by reacting to my husband's every mood change. Each mood shift would put me on high alert. I was making myself crazy trying to adapt my feelings to the possible meaning of each new mood. I'm sure that was very frustrating for my husband to experience. After we had hit three years of trying to recover, he was the first to say that my feelings and actions were totally justified. But I know I can keep improving my behaviors by learning better ways to respond. I was doing the best I could with what I knew, but I still take accountability for my actions and what I caused because of what I didn't know. Even though I knew nothing else, and was deep into trauma, I still can become better. And I don't have to keep treating him like that with unhealthy responses. I needed to change my patterns as I learned and healed. I wish the same thing from my husband. As he learns new ways, I will see the changes. Loving him on a deep level is happening. I continue to work really hard to achieve this. If I can do it, I will lead a life of love, forgiveness, and true faith in God. I will come to love my husband for his spirit in the same way the Savior loves him. My husband is worth it. We all are. Living in love is the person I want to be and the person I will be.

This has brought me so much peace. Now that I've gained some peace, I don't like when it leaves. That feeling means everything to me. I missed it for so long trying to navigate through this crazy mess. Now that I have finally learned how to get it, I do everything I can to keep it. That true peace is a rest from the weary days I've had. It is a gift, a spiritual gift. Being able to see God's hand giving me that peace has been a revelation. Why would I want to live any part of my day without Heavenly Father and the Savior by my side? I don't! That spiritual connection through peace showed me how real our relationship with Heaven is and how close it is. It is right there, just above our head. That's how I feel and see it. Help is a moment away.

Unfortunately, we tend to go about our day by ourselves when we have access to the living God! How have I missed this truth all these years! Our very best friends that love us more than any person on earth are a single second away. Yet it's taken me this long to realize this. They are right there. Every time I let them in and really listen, they have the answers. It takes my obedience to follow their counsel. When I do, I see before my eyes that everything falls into place as it should be. Then, I have peace. I get so scared sometimes that I'm being told something that isn't going to work. But I'm not doing any better navigating on my own, so I just need to listen to the one being that actually does know all.

I imagine a large puzzle placed on a table in front of me. The bottom edge is put together along with two pieces going up the middle. I'm looking at all the other pieces thinking, "How am I going to do this? There are 5,000 pieces. There's no way I can put this together. I cannot see how I'm going to make this work." Plus, to make it more complicated, there's no box with the picture of what it's supposed to look like. How is this possible? I constantly fall into the trap of thinking I need to see the whole puzzle to be able to put the pieces together. I am always going back to Heavenly Father saying, "I just need the details. I will do what you ask, but can you first show me how it's all going to play out? That would be so much easier for me to handle." Instead, Heavenly Father says, "The great thing is you don't need to see the whole picture. Just concentrate on the piece I give you, find where it fits, feel your accomplishment that you found where it goes, then come back and ask me how to find the next piece. The big picture is actually quite big and if I show you, you will get caught up in all the little details. You will still question me on how this is all supposed to work, but trust me, this is the best way. I give you a piece, we celebrate when you finish it, and we repeat. It's a great plan."

In the scriptures it states, "Trust in God with all thine heart and lean not unto thine own understanding. In all thy ways acknowledge him and he shall direct thy path" (Proverbs 3:5-6). It takes strict obedience. This is a daily practice. Reaching that place where you can say to yourself, "I'm tired of directing my life. I give it to you, God. I want nothing more than to do only what you want from me. I desire nothing else. If you are telling me what to do, I know I will be happier than I could ever be by trying to control everything around me.

This helps me to take things one day at a time. I'm always trying to get ahead of myself. Heavenly Father constantly has to remind me that I only need to do one thing at a time. I only need to know one thing at a time. I don't have to see the whole picture. That's been the hardest lesson for me. I want to see the whole picture placed before me. That way, I could assess what needs to be done. I could put a plan in place. I would feel a sense of security knowing what I was signing up for. This way of thinking makes sense if I want to run my life and be the one in charge of it. But if I want Him to direct it, then He's the only one who gets to know the plan. I have cried so many nights wishing to understand the unknown. It's paralyzing. It takes every ounce of sanity I have and deflates my last bit of energy. It steals away my peace. The unknown is a never-ending abyss of all the possible things that could happen. My unknown covers all the issues that would come up if we divorced. It takes over my mind as I list in my head all that could go wrong. Let me tell you, I have envisioned a lot of things! The list of possibilities is probably endless. One day I finally said, "The craziness has to stop! I have to get out of my head."

I began my journey seeking true healing. What does that mean? What does it look like? What do I do? Where do I start? I had reached my rock bottom when I had cut my husband's ties. I was screaming at the top of my lungs at him to tell me the truth. "I can't handle the lies anymore!" He yelled back with, "No! I will never tell you anything." My heart was racing as he spoke in that way to me. I was a disaster. I needed immediate help. I called my wonderful friend, who is also a recovering and healing spouse of an addict. She had personally done the 12 steps through S-Anon, a support group for relatives and friends of sexually addicted people. This group uses the big blue book for AA, Alcoholics Anonymous, to help members heal from their loved ones' sexual addictions. I had already purchased the book months previous. I had read some, but hadn't committed to the process yet.

I called my friend and said, "I'm ready."

She answered, "Are you sure? Is there anything left you can think of that you can do to help him or yourself?"

I said, "I've tried everything I can think of. I have nothing left."

She said, "Good. You are ready. You are not ready if you still think you can try one more thing."

I assured her I had nothing left. So we began. She spent many hours with me going through the steps. We cried together as we read about submitting to God because we could not manage this anymore on our own. It was a cleansing and beautiful experience. I love my friend. I love the service she gave me. I feel deep gratitude that she did something for me that I could not do for myself. This was the start of my journey of finding my real healing. The steps taught me that I could no longer think the way I had in the past. I had to create a new way of thinking if I wanted to achieve healing and return to peace and love in my heart.

I then used the LDS Addiction Recovery Program (ARP) to solidify principles to aid in the spiritual nature of my healing. My testimony continued to grow each week as I discussed with other women letting go and letting God heal us. I love those women like they are family. We have a bond the minute we meet for the first time. We share something so personal and so devastating, that there is instant care and love for each other. These women truly know me. They see the raw feelings that are deep in my core. Together we rise as we comfort, guide, and follow the principles spelled out in the steps. There is absolute healing available to us.

I want to say more about my desire to see the whole plan. I now know that seeing it all at once would kill me. I wouldn't be able to take it all in. If I had known 20 years ago what I know now, I would have run as fast as I could the other way. I most likely would have married another person just like my husband. I needed this time to learn one thing at a time and step by step, the plan for my life. I needed to gain knowledge from each piece of the puzzle along the way. I wouldn't change it for anything. I have learned so much about the Savior, the blessings from going to my church's temple each week, and praying my guts out for all of these years. I needed this path for my very own refinement. I needed to become Me. This was the only way. Heavenly Father knew this. That is why He gets to be in charge. That's why each morning I submit my will and selfish desires to Him so He can give me the step for that day. I love Him. I love that He is trying to help me love myself and love my husband. He knows how great my husband is. I know how great he is. He is the best guy. That guy just so happens to be trapped inside the cage of addiction. I believe that all our addicted love ones are, in their core, great people. They are in there. It is the most frustrating thing to try and break them out. You cut through a bar and reach your hand in to get them to take yours so you can lead them out. But they inch backward. You cut open another bar and lean your entire body in and, yet, they still back themselves in the corner and don't walk out. It is senseless craziness. It is the weirdest, shake your head back-and-forth, mind-blowing experience, to watch your loved one not get it. It's awful to see them not even slightly grasp the simple words you are saying to them.

"Just walk out of the cell. Just walk. That's it. Move your legs forward."

But they look at you like you are speaking a foreign language. That's why I did the steps for myself. I had to step away from making him do anything. I needed to walk out of my own cell. I created my own cell by thinking things had to look and be a certain way. I couldn't see. I couldn't hear the simple words God told me.

"Walk away. Walk out of this crazy circle. Move forward on your own path."

I needed to see that our minds don't think alike. Both of us are broken for different reasons. We couldn't help each other. I wanted him to help me and let me help him. I learned the hard way to let go and only do the work for me. That saved me. Healing me through God restored my peace and sanity. I love life again. I feel peace. I never want to let it go. Prayer has taken over my life so that I can let God lead the way. I've said prayers by my bed, prayers in my closet, in my bathroom, in the kitchen, and in my car. I've poured out prayers at church and on the treadmill…prayers, prayers, prayers.

If you have felt lost from God, turn back to Him by offering a prayer. He is still there for you. He loves you. You don't have to be perfect for Him to help you. Trust me, I've messed up lots on this road, but He has never left. Sometimes I have disconnected, but He never has. When I'm unsure, I listen to peaceful, spiritual, and uplifting music. Doing that comforts my mind and heart. It's how I feel His love.

CHAPTER 12

Chain Links

When our kids were little we told them about a trip we were planning. It was a Disney cruise. They were jumping, laughing, and full of excitement. They had never been on a cruise before and they could hardly contain themselves. We told them the date and they quickly got out the calendar to see how many days until we left. They disappeared for hours and came back with 78 links of construction paper chained together. They hung it on the wall and took turns every day tearing off a link. Each week they would enthusiastically say, "Only 70 more days...only 45 days"...all the way to the night before we left.

Through this experience, I have found that I often say to Heavenly Father, "How many more days?" How many days until I feel whole, or till he's better, or...or...or...? Are we there yet? Are we there yet? Are we there yet?"

118

Lovingly, He guides me through each step. As I make it through, I am filled with more love and desire to live righteously, to become more, and to do all that my Father asks of me. Each time I tear off a chain link of learning, I feel better and more excited. Each day as the chains fall off, I am different. I keep changing with every step I take toward God. I am excited for the future when I will meet my God face to face. He has given me life and saved me from the pain of this addiction. He has brought me out. Not just because he wanted to. He could certainly do that, but He gave me the opportunity to want Him, ask Him, and come to Him. Then, as I gave Him one hand and then the other, He gave me everything.

I am overjoyed with excitement as the chains have almost dissolved. I no longer desire to turn back to the life I once knew. I can see that the waiting and working on each chain was for my benefit. How could I truly be excited and yearn for my next portion of life, my "Disney cruise," if I didn't know why I should be excited? If my kids had never seen commercials or heard of others going on a cruise they wouldn't have had the same reaction. Instead, they planned by searching online about the great adventures this trip would give them.

As I have used all of the resources revealed to me, I now know what my life can look like. That knowledge feels great! I'm full of anticipation for the next stage. I'm not talking about my marriage, because honestly as I continue with my face toward God, I am not sure if we will be together in the future. The next stage will be full of healthy living. I know who I am! I know that my feelings, inspirations, and decisions are good. I am worth it! And I know that his issues have nothing to do with me. Even when he tries to take me down in an addictive cycle, I am prepared. I have done the work and I am on stable footing. God is my partner. I will not trust in the arm of the flesh. One of the greatest chains that broke was the one of second guessing my feelings and intuition. God will never lead me astray. I no longer wonder if it's my thoughts or His. I recognize Him. If I ever question that, He answers me on the spot. I continue working on me and my relationship with God. I continue praying every day that my husband will do the same. If he knew what he was missing, he would run full force and never look back. But, until he gains that desire to give up his own will, the chains he carries will remain intact and used as a force against him. His recovery and healing are between him and God. Do I hope that he makes it? Yes! Do I want to live an eternal life with him? I want nothing more. Do I believe he can do it? Absolutely!

He is stronger than he realizes and he's filled with so much love that's waiting to take over his life. I couldn't have loved him any more through all this. I am grateful I was taught so much beautiful truth about God and His eternal plan. I am stronger than my husband thinks. With God on my side, I can handle all that he throws at me. And if he decides to release control, his life will be better than ever.

It is difficult learning to accept the ups and downs of the new lessons we need to learn. I was trying to calmly, but assertively, talk to my husband about a triggering moment for me in a movie we were watching. This was something we had been working on in counseling. We were to be aware of how we were feeling at all times. We were learning how to stay in the present. We had been invited to communicate each time we noticed a change in our emotions. I was using the "I feel" phrase and working to keep calm. He sat there listening, but didn't have anything to say in response.

I asked if any of this made sense and if his brain understood what I was saying. He looked a bit blank, but not rude in the way he had responded in the past. That was progress. I recognized this and thought, "Okay, well, he's not putting up a wall so this is good!" I again asked if he understood or if I explained it clearly. He finally just said, "Yes, I heard you." And then nothing. I waited and looked at him with an, "Is there anything else?" look and he continued with, "I love you," and gave a kissy face. "I'm sorry you felt bothered."

My love language is to hear kind and loving words of affirmation. His language is hugs and affection. I've talked with him about this. We will both have our needs met if he can show me my love language instead of giving me his love language. When I am having a deep conversation with him or I'm bothered, I want him to stay a bit back, listen to my words, and acknowledge he heard me. It makes me feel crazy when he immediately gets close to me, hugging me all over and doesn't say a word. I freak out. It feels to me like, "Let's pretend this didn't happen" and "No, I don't want to listen to how you feel or what's going on with you." Knowing his loving nature, I'm sure some of that is truth. He doesn't like confrontation and has the mindset of "can't we just all get along." But the other side of it is that he is trying to show me that even though things are terrible, he still cares for me. When I feel heard and validated, I automatically want to hug and love. His validation and connection comes from physical affection. It's a catch-22.

One day I wanted to talk to him about some things and I sensed it may not go well. I was in a good place and full of peace. So I wanted to try something new. I tried to give him what he needed before I even started talking. So in the kitchen I went up to him and just embraced him. I hugged him for real and tried to really connect with him on a spiritual level. His spirit is in there, so I thought of loving his spirit and not worrying about the mixed-up feelings I have for his earthly state of being. I thought loving thoughts toward his spirit.

I kissed him, rubbed his back, and then kindly said, "Hey, I'd like to talk to you for a few minutes. Is that okay?"

He said, "Yes, of course!"

We sat on the couch and had a really great open conversation of where we both were, what was working, and what needed improvement. He talked a lot, giving me the words I needed to hear and then we finished up with more hugs and lots of love for one another. All this time, I felt like he should go first. If he talked to me with words then naturally I will feel his love and want to be affectionate toward him. That was the first day that it hit me that I could go first. I could set the tone for the conversation and we both left feeling validated and full of love. I am learning so many things. God is showing me my weaknesses and where I need improvement. This was one of them. The other one is learning to accept where he is. When we had the first conversation about the triggering scene in the movie, I left shaking my head in disapproval that he doesn't get it. I tried explaining it in different ways but he couldn't grasp it. It's frustrating to watch someone clearly not get something that feels so basic.

The next morning as I pondered through that event, I realized once again that no amount of repeating the same thing over and over is going to help someone understand. He can't understand because HE CAN'T UNDERSTAND. He really can't! His brain cells are not connected to this concept. As frustrating as it is, I have to accept that if he could, he would! But, he can't. So I took a deep breath and thanked God for showing me this weakness of mine. I reminded myself, like I frequently do, that it is line upon line and one step at a time. His steps are not the same as my steps. By noticing the changes, I can see the work is moving forward. He is now grasping things that he was unable to understand a year ago. I have faith and hope that as he stays in recovery, he'll have brain connections. Acceptance is my new goal. It feels eye-opening to have learned this. It will be so much help for me to keep peace in my soul when my words don't mean anything to him. This will let me release these harmful chains.

I'm committed to talking to him about the things I'm inspired to say. If he stares blankly, I will respond with, "Well, maybe it's something to think about. I just wanted to let you know what's going on with me." It sounds good as I write it. Now I need the strength to conquer. I will not give up. I will fight the fight. Being this far into recovery has actually brought out a love for this fight. I love the things I'm learning. I appreciate that I get to change my weaknesses and not be hindered by them anymore. Each time I overcome something that was dragging me down, I feel another burden lifted and another chain broken. And I feel strong, empowered, and brave. I like it. I like the person I am becoming.

CHAPTER 13

Seeing the Face of God

My God always comes through. He reassured me this next step was right. It felt like my fate was hanging in the balance awaiting his decision. It had been a few months into our separation and two weeks since giving my husband a deadline of agreeing to some changes. During this time, I've only heard backlash from him. He was mad about the timeframe. He kept saying it's an ultimatum and he is not going to listen. Throughout the two weeks, we were on the edge of divorce multiple times. It was so sad to watch my marriage and family falling apart. Each time I felt the despair, I went to the Lord, asking if this was the right plan. I wanted to know if I was following it correctly. I would get reassurance and approval that I was doing what was asked. So I kept on. It was hard to listen to my husband fight with me about the boundary. It was breaking my heart that he was ready to give up everything. He was letting me go. How could he do this? I have fought for him and our marriage for 20 years!

I had always been the one in charge of making sure we made it. I didn't realize that truth until this experience. It didn't matter how much I fought for him, he never fought for me. It was a one-sided relationship. It had been this way since our first day of marriage. My heart was breaking, yet I was as strong as ever. I was lifted and guided. I hurt because my husband couldn't see. He didn't know his truth. All he could see was the pain and work that would be in his future if he fought for his life and our marriage.

Oddly enough, even though he was not "all in," he still had this drive to do certain things that were bringing us together. He asked me three times that week to listen with him to segments of "Your Brain on Love" by Stan Tatkin. This was a series given to us by our counselor to help build intimacy and connection on all levels. Each time there were "aha moments" for both of us. For me, I felt validated in my feelings in wanting an emotional connection. For him, he received moments of "Oh, that's how I'm treating her and I need to change that behavior." It was really good but also painful to watch him go back and forth from acceptance to justification. The day we listened, he was kind and showed care and concern for me in our situation. But it didn't last. Sometimes I got to see this person for a few hours and sometimes for the entire day. But by the next morning, he had talked himself out of wanting to do the necessary work. Then we were back to talking divorce and him stating he will never give up his desires. It was a crazy roller coaster.

He would need to come to counseling with his plan on what changes he was going to make and how he planned to accomplish them. I needed to see that he desired to be better. I needed to know that he understood the impact on me. It was essential that if he wanted our family, he needed to accept that there would be no more blaming. He needed to be accountable for his actions and strive to become a reliable and honest partner. A few days before that meeting, tension was high and I kept shaking my head to the Lord saying, "I can't see how this is going to work. He is so prideful and unwilling. Are you sure this is the plan?"

I met with my church bishop and he asked if he could fast with me. We decided Tuesday would work and I invited my mom and siblings to do this with us. They have been such a huge support for me. They are kind and loving. They love both me and my husband so much. We fasted and prayed diligently. They sent me scriptures, conference talks, and words of inspiration. It was amazing. They can see the good in him and they understand this is a fight against Satan, not against my husband. We were all fighting for him. Two days before the meeting things were still not good. One day, he would say he'd try, and the next he would be bombarded with evil influence. I could see him wrestling with this decision.

While in my church house I had a beautiful experience and was told to let go of my control. I needed to stop trying to fix everything. I didn't need to tell him one more reason he should try or give him any advice about how he would ruin our family if he didn't choose to fight. I was told to back up so that Heavenly Father and the Savior could do their work. It has been so hard for me to learn this. I constantly am taking back the control. He doesn't want to hear from me because right now he doesn't even like me. That means nothing I say will be accepted. So it does more damage than good. I listened. I backed away, and let God do His work.

My family and I continued praying and fighting. Each morning I asked in prayer what my part could be that day. I ended up at my church temple three days in a row. That was my part. I could pray, receive strength for my own soul, and plead on my husband's behalf. Overnight his heart softened. He came to our counseling appointment with a plan. He cried as he read it and committed to being a kind and loving husband. Our counselor pressed him on specifics and made sure he understood that this plan was a plan of action and not just written words. He told me that even though he was initially mad about the deadline, he was grateful. It gave him the opportunity to look inside himself, pray, and decide what he wanted in his life. He said he wanted our family. I'm cautiously optimistic that he will do the work.

For now I am grateful to learn these very hard lessons. I have learned so much and I can see how giving up my control and letting God do the work is so much better. I drag out the learning when I take over and continue to get in my own way. The journey is excruciatingly painful. Only those who have walked it know what I mean. There are no words sufficient to express the heartache one feels going through this craziness. Gratefully, the blessings far outweigh the devastation. I knew I needed to keep going. I had to endure the entire trial to receive this gift. Many times I wanted to give up. So many days were way too hard. Instead of turning away from God and giving up, I turned toward Him and gave in. I gave up my pride. I told Him I could not do this anymore. And, because I went to the right source with my pain and anger, He showed me the way out.

Our counseling appointment could have gone either way. But the two days that I backed away and let God handle the details, I experienced complete peace and joy. Never could I have imagined feeling so complete and loved in those moments of uncertainty. Only God and His angels could give me that. I could only accept His peace when I stopped my own agenda and let Him work. He is a miracle worker. He has worked miracles in me. I can't wait to see Him face-to-face and hug Him as tight as I can.

Seeing the face of God will be the greatest day of my existence. How does one go about seeing the face of our Lord and Savior? In the scriptures it states that anyone can see His face. This is not reserved just for prophets and apostles of old or even modern-day church leaders. It clearly states what is required to see the face of the Only Begotten.

Again, I think of Job. He really was an amazing person to have gone through such hardship without any relief. He still chose God. He didn't lose sight. He didn't turn away. He taught us that he would give all for God. He would even give his life. His children were taken from him, his livelihood, his wealth, status in his community and then finally his health. He was covered in boils all over his body. He was in severe pain emotionally, physically, and mentally.

But spiritually he didn't waiver. Why? How? He knew that there was someone bigger than him who was in control. He had no need to fight for his rights or demand restitution from God for taking away everything he had in his life. He didn't feel the pride well up in his heart and curse the world. He didn't hate his friends for turning against him. They all thought he was crazy for standing by God. "How could your God let this happen to you?" Why do you still believe in him? You're crazy!" Instead in humility, Job turned to the God that let all these terrible things happen and offer up his gratitude for being there for him during these hard trials. These were tests of faith that I hope to never endure. I can't begin to imagine his pain. He trusted the Lord. He trusted that all would be made right if he kept his faith and laid his burdens at the feet of the Lord.

What does that mean to lay your burdens at the feet of the Lord? To me, it means to bring Him everything—my whole entire heart. Give Him the aching pain, the agony of despair, and the anger, hate, and resentment. It means to bring the turmoil along with drops of faith that He is going to hear my prayers and help me through. I have seen this.

I have experienced death in my own right. Even though I'm not Job, it doesn't mean my journey has not been hard. It has felt impossible. But as I laid my pain in front of the Savior, He has shown me how to survive. He has given me peace and love even through the fire of death. I have felt him cradle me in His arms and talk softly of my worth and my divinity. He quietly told me that He has a plan for me. He reassured that even though He will not stop people, particularly my husband, from hurting me and causing pain to my soul, He will be there to show me the way out. He will guide gently through the thicket of thorns and briars. He will not save me from the cuts I receive as I walk. But, if I slowly take each step holding tightly to His hand, He will never let go. I just need to hold His hand and move on the path He is walking before me.

How do I see the face of God? I follow Him. I serve Him. I never give up. When I fall, I get back up and go to Him. I ask for forgiveness and help. As we grow in our faith, we may see His face through the tender mercies that come our way. For those who continue to do all that is asked, no matter how hard the task, they will actually see the face of God. They will have proven that even when asked to do hard things, they will do His will. By so doing, they will be promised the kingdom. Any one of us can gain that promise. It says so in scripture. It says so in talks given by our apostles. I've read them over and over again. I find hope and beauty in reading those words. Even in this fallen state, we can receive this promise.

When my son was 18 years old he came home from a church seminary class and boldly asked me if I have seen the face of God. I was shocked and taken a back and asked why he would ask me that? He began telling me all he learned that day about having your calling and election made sure. He told me all the promises he learned and that even those who have seen His face will still make mistakes because we live this earthly life. But if they repent then they are good to go and going to the celestial kingdom in heaven. I loved his excitement as he relayed everything he learned. I loved his testimony and the light in his eyes as he knew he was speaking truth to me about what he learned. It was one of those moments when you thank Heavenly Father that He is helping you take care of your family.

A few years ago, I followed this concept with my children. I gave them to God and admitted in prayer that I had been trying to control their every move. I was so fearful of what mistakes they might make that would ruin their lives and I was going crazy. He whispered the reminder and asked, "How did you know to choose the Lord? How did you become the person you are now?" It was because I made big mistakes that brought me to a turning point. I had to ask myself, "Which way do I turn, to the world or the Lord?" I chose the Lord. Those experiences increased my faith and testimony in what I now know is right. My children need that same thing. That day, years ago, I laid my children at the feet of my Savior. He took them. I pray for them, I teach them what I learn, and I show by example how to be a follower of Christ. I'm hopeful that through their trials they will also choose the path of God.

That day as my son spoke, I saw God showing him truth by telling him these things are true. It was amazing. My daughter, who was 15 at the time, watched in awe as he spoke with such clarity. I could see her mouth wide open turning her head to me then back to him. She felt the truth in his words. When she attends that church class, she too will learn these wonderful truths that we are not alone and we can live righteously and someday see the face of God.

CHAPTER 14

Heaven Help Me!

I wasn't aware how much heaven and earth truly intertwine until this experience. When I fall to my knees blurting out, "I don't know what to do." When I'm rocking back and forth, hands over my face, shaking my head and repeating, "I can't do this, I don't know how. This is bigger than me. Please help me." Screaming, "I don't know how to do this!" What happens? Who comes to my aid? And how do they? There have been times I've been on my knees racked with torment for hours. In those moments I feel like I am losing grasp of my reality. I am too overwhelmed with my situation or the task at hand.

I'm learning the balance between taking care of me, and having the patience with this addiction. There are things I want right now. Or yesterday would have been nice. How do I heal, practice self-care, and still trust that recovery for him is not on my timetable? How do I respect my need for a certain level of progression for me to sanely and safely stay in this marriage? It's extremely difficult for me. I am one that, when given a task, I will look at it, analyze it, plan my attack, and then go for it. This has been no different. When I notice that I am full of hate, I figure out why. I put my safety plan in place and execute a plan to achieve success. But addiction cannot be controlled like this. Every plan can be put in place, but addiction likes the control. The addict himself likes the control, not over the addiction, but over the "hows" and "whens" of recovery. He likes to tell me how much he will do and that I should be okay with it. Yes, I agree that he can choose his path. As do I.

I choose to not live in chaos and emotional abuse. If he chooses tiny bits of recovery then I will continue to experience more emotional trauma. If he doesn't value me as his wife, whom he committed to cherish, then I choose to not have him in my life. Recently, he has been up against everything I say. In my mind, I picture his two fists, chest level, and thumbs upward. Each time I tell him, "I feel this when you do that," I see them clinch a little tighter. Every time I explain how it feels when he doesn't consider me part of his team, I see the fist get tighter. I am his greatest advocate, yet he sees me as his worst enemy. If I suggest it, ask for it, or cry for it, he is automatically against it and becomes resentful. If his counselor or our church bishop suggests it, he says he will try. We have discussed this together in therapy. He is unsure why he does this, but he still does. I am at a turning point.

I have done my healing. I feel good about where I am and whom I've become. I look daily at what I still need to improve on. There are still lots of weaknesses. But I feel really good about what I accomplished working my recovery for those three years. I don't want him in my life anymore if he can't jump on board with treating me with love, kindness, respect, and selflessness. It's coming down to the end. He needs to decide. He told me that it will be my choice if I can't live with him. It's not about me keeping the marriage together. I can't work his recovery for him. I've done my work. I paved my own side of the street. Now I'm sitting on the curb waiting to see if he will cross the street. I can't go get him. I can't go on his side of the street. There is a clear line of where I belong and I've learned the painful truth that I don't belong on his side of the street. I do all my work from my side, and he does his work on his side. Then, if we both do that, we will end at the top of the road where they join together and become one road. Right now, I'm at the top of the road where it's almost to the joining point. He's nowhere to be found. What is he going to do? I don't know. All I can do is let him know that I'm here.

I want a partner for life to work with me. I hope he chooses that same thing. The hurtful part is watching him choose himself as he deliberately does things he knows hurt me. The looks of daggers and jabs of blame are unacceptable. The look he has on his face as I ask for him to show me love brings tears to my eyes. It breaks my heart that I say, "Please love me," and he can't. I was trying to talk to him one night and he could not hear me. He was resentful and distant. He blames me for my feelings. But you know what? I can feel sad! I can feel upset by his actions! I'm tired of him rationalizing his behavior and blame shifting. It is nonsense and so hurtful. Things have got to change. I don't think he's sober. But I can't really know that. All I see is what he does, how he acts, and how he responds to me. It's all addict behavior. It had gotten worse and felt like the same pattern as the past. Our marriage can't last if he continues to lie. At some point, he needs to reach a point of honesty to remain with me. I don't know when or if that will come. I know Heavenly Father will tell me. So far, He just tells me I'm not emotionally safe with him, so I need to protect myself with boundaries. That's what I'm doing. Protecting myself does help me feel so much better.

There have been so many pivotal moments in this journey. I've been asked, yet again, to do something extremely difficult. Not by my husband or my counselor, not by my bishop or my family members, but by God. He's asked me to do something that could be so painful. It could end all that I've known. I'm nervous, anxious, and stressed. Not about what I have to do, but about the outcome. My bishop gave me a blessing. Afterwards, he was prompted to share a talk with me. He turned it on and for 10 minutes we listened. It's called "But If Not... " by Elder Dennis Simmons, from the April LDS General Conference 2004. The talk is about having the faith to do whatever God asks. Do we have the faith to trust God and do His will when we don't know the outcome? I have to believe that when He asks me to do something, He will take care of me and all will be right. I cling to the hope that everything will work out because I listened. My hopes and dreams will come true because I did all that He asked of me. But it's also having the faith that if He does not fix everything and make it better, I will still choose Him. If he asks me to enforce a boundary that results in divorce, will I still choose Him?

As I listened to this talk, tears fell from my eyes. I do have the faith necessary to do hard things. I listen and I obey. God always has shown me what to do and has always taken care of me. But right now, at this very moment, if I do this expecting that once again He will change my husband's heart, but that doesn't happen, will I still trust Him? Will I still immediately fall to my knees and thank Him for walking this path with me? Will I continue to submit my will and do all that is asked and required? "But if not" means I have faith that good things will come; but if not, will I turn away from God? I trust that miracles will happen in my life and my specific prayers will be answered. But if not, will I continue believing that God hears me and wants to help and guide me? The answer is "Yes." It's yes because of what I know... He knows more. He knows what I want. He knows if that's what I need. My plan is not His plan. He knows more. If all is taken from me, I still choose Him. By doing that, I am telling my God that I know and trust that He has a plan for me. That plan may look different or feel different than what I thought should happen for me and my family, but He knows all.

God loves me. He loves my family. He doesn't want to inflict pain on us. What He does want is for us to come to Him so He can make us more. My pain can become my strength. My willingness to give up everything is the only way to let Him show me what He wants for me. He has taught me how to trust Him. He didn't ask me to do something this hard at first. He asked small things. As I followed, He asked more of me. He showed me I could trust him. He never steered me wrong. It's never happened. As I listen, He guides. As I follow, He blesses.

One year into recovery I was praying by my bed. Things were really bad. I did not know why. Nothing felt right or good. I felt crazy. Emotionally I felt lost and didn't know what to do. My husband was professing his sobriety and making me feel terrible about my feelings. I was breaking and I didn't know why things were so hard for me. Why couldn't I get past this? Why was I dying when he was in recovery? As I prayed and poured my heart out to God, the words were spoken more clearly in my mind than I had ever heard before.

Heavenly Father said, *"He needs to leave. Not separation. Not divorce. But he needs to go somewhere for a couple of weeks so you can have a reprieve and he can figure out what he should be doing."* This was huge for me. I had never asked him to leave in my life! I had asked him a couple of times to sleep on the couch, but he never would! If I needed space, I had to be the one to leave. Now Heavenly Father was telling me to ask him to leave the house?

I was panicked. In prayer I said, "If he leaves, he will have no one."

"He will have me," He responded.

"What if he doesn't choose you?" I questioned.

"He's not choosing me right now anyway," came the reply.

My heart sank. It really did. I was devastated that this was my answer. I could not see how this was going to play out. It took me a few days of processing it. I knew that I had heard words from that prayer. I knew that He specifically asked me to do this. I knew I had to be obedient. As I thought through the alternative of staying in this crazy emotional life, I knew I couldn't do that either. So I trusted.

I told my husband, "I'm not sure what it means exactly, or where you're supposed to go. I'd love if you'd work on it with your counselor, come up with a plan, and then we will talk about it." It worked. He agreed. And Heavenly Father healed my wounded heart that week. What I didn't know was that my husband had not been sober that entire year. I didn't know that him leaving would mean two weeks of using, contacting his online affairs, and acting out. If I knew that information, it would have hindered what I needed for me at that time. Heavenly Father was giving me what I needed at that exact moment. My heart needed a break. I needed to be able to breathe, by myself, in my own space. He knew my husband was in full relapse and had never been sober. But that didn't matter at that point. I wasn't ready to deal with that and my husband wasn't either.

Heavenly Father works in His timing. His timing benefits us both. That experience showed me that even when I'm scared to do His will, He will take care of me if I'm obedient. This small act on my part opened the door to more of these opportunities. I say opportunities because even though they feel like death at the time, the blessings that I've received from following Him have been undeniable.

The following year, April 2014, I would again be asked to do something hard. This time he had to get out of the house or check in to a rehab center. He had gotten worse. Things were so bad that I couldn't even handle being around him. He argued that he was sober and I was crazy. He told me I needed medication and I was wrong. The Spirit kept telling me that he was being dishonest, that things were not good, and this time it was over. No more could this keep going on. It was now or never. I stated, "You get the help you need or get out." He freaked out. I was so sure in my conviction that I just calmly said, "I'm sorry. But I do not believe you."

It had taken me over a week to finally be able to confront him about all this. It was a week of constantly praying and pleading with God that this couldn't be. He was asking me to possibly break up my family. What about my children? What about our marriage? But He kept assuring me that this was supposed to be. This had to happen. I remember praying in my closet. I felt like I was ready to tell him. I accepted and told Heavenly Father I was ready. I walked out of my closet and out my bedroom door. I had maybe walked 10 seconds when I turned right around again and went back into my closet.

"I can't do this," I cried to Heavenly Father. "I don't know how to do this. Please help me." Again, He reassured me and I felt warm love from the Savior surround my shoulders. I could do this. I could do something crazy because my Heavenly Father was in charge. I did it. And it was awful. This happened on a Monday.

My husband said he would choose divorce, but he would wait one week until the following Monday to tell the kids. I'm not sure why he chose that, but I didn't care. I was grateful.

I then said, "Okay, Heavenly Father, we've got one week to change his heart." I called in a prayer intervention to my family and his. I let them know that we needed to fight for him. I told them he was in a bad place and ready to give up his family. We needed to pull out all the stops for him. So, the week began, and we fasted and prayed. I spent hours in my church's temple, and even more hours on my knees. It was intense. I knew not to say a single word to him about anything. I left him alone. This was crucial. I was fighting against Satan and I needed to do everything quietly with God.

Sunday night came and there were no changes. He was as cold and hard-hearted as ever. I sobbed in my closet, "How can this be? How can the decisions of one person affect an entire family of good people?" I felt so devastated.

At that moment, my phone buzzed. My brother had texted me. It boldly said, "Don't worry, angels are on their way." Oh, my goodness. I felt it. Chills covered my skin and peace filled my heart. My body calmed and relaxed as I got in bed. I lay there on my back staring up at the dark ceiling. Sure enough, the Spirit was strong and quietly my husband began to talk. He started expressing his feelings. He said he did want to try. I watched as the darkness lifted. I witnessed a true miracle happening before my eyes. He agreed to check in to rehab. I was shocked and ever so grateful. All week I had second-guessed my prompting to have him leave. I had gone back and forth on the answer I had received. Every time I questioned, I went back to the Lord and asked Him. He reassured me every time that what I was doing was correct.

The next day I called my brother and asked why he sent the text about angels? He said, "The craziest thing happened. I was brushing my teeth when all of the sudden I heard a voice yell out, *"Your sister needs you!"* So I grabbed my wife and our mom (who was visiting at the time) and I said, "This is it. She needs us and we need to pray like we have never prayed before."

And so it was. Angels came to our rescue.

Later, after my husband came out of rehab, I told him of the prayer intervention and the experience with my brother.

He said, "I believe that! That night in bed I physically felt evil leaving me." He said he had made a pact with himself at the beginning of the week that he would not change. He would not listen to me and would never go to rehab. But God intervened. He heard our prayers of faith. He accepted the family fast. God helped my husband in a way he could accept. He became humble and did the Lord's will. It was the most amazing testimony-building thing I have ever witnessed.

These experiences testify to me that God does know what needs to happen. I have no choice but to listen when He asks me to do hard things. I know that the blessings of obedience come in ways I don't even expect or comprehend.

Once again, I am in the middle of something hard. I had to confront my husband again. He has a few days to decide what he will do. Will he submit all and go all in, or will he flee because it's too hard? I do not know. I've asked Heavenly Father if He's sure this is what He wants me to do. He has said over and over that, "Yes, this is the next step." So again, I've spent the majority of my time on my knees in prayer, driving in prayer, walking in prayer, and sitting in church in prayer. I received a blessing today for added strength. My family is standing by me to pray and fast on my husband's behalf.

Why do I stay? Why do I keep doing this? The answer is because God has asked me to. I love my husband more than anything. I hate addiction. I hate the lies and deception that comes along with it. But I don't hate my husband. I'm sad and hurt for him that he can't see clearly. I know he will recover. I really do. I'm hopeful it's with me so together we can rise and receive the blessings that would be ours when we reach the top. The end is still up in the air. But I will keep fighting for him, for us, and for my family, until Heavenly Father says, "No more." When He says to me, "You did all I asked and there's nothing more you can do," then I will walk away.

Until then, I will continue with hope that the angels of heaven will surround my husband in light and love. I pray he will see himself, he will see me, and he will see how great life can be by giving up all and following God's path for him.

CHAPTER 15

Be Still

One thing that has been hard for me is to "be still" and let God do the work. One experience stands out. My daughter had a school choir concert the same night that my son had his end-of-the-year tennis party and awards night. My husband took the kids and went to the party and I went to the concert. I was by myself sitting in my own row: I was spiraling that day. I don't remember the specifics of what I was dealing with. But I do know that I could hardly breathe. It was taking everything I had to function that day. I know my husband and I were not in a good place, but that happens a lot, so this was just one of those days. I remember feeling grateful I got to be at the school alone watching my daughter. It was nice. I sat and closed my eyes as I waited for it to start. I also read the scriptures. My heart was pounding and I was trying to calm my fears and anxieties.

The concert began and I prayed, "Please, God, tell me what my next step is. Tell me what I should be working on." I instantly heard, "Be still. Just be still."

I furrowed my brow. What? Be still? I can't be still! How do you "be still?" I don't know how to be still. After all these questions ran through my mind, I started processing through why I didn't know how to be still. The thoughts came. I've never been still. Being still means I'm not working! I'm a doer. Each time something needs to be done, I am on it! I've carried the burden and job of making sure all is well. Being still means I'm not doing my part or doing all I can! Then, if something bad happens, I am to blame. It was shown to me that those thoughts were control. I couldn't be still because I didn't feel in control of everything.

I thought that if I was tirelessly working and things still didn't happen, at least I did my part and I'd have no regrets. But that's not entirely true. It's about intentions. If I'm working hard to make sure I don't get hurt then that's control. If I'm working to submit all and follow God's plan, then that's different.

I sat for a moment, scared to death! I honestly did not know how to be still. I took a big breath and let it out.

I asked my Father in Heaven, "How do I do this? I really don't even have the concept or know how in my brain. I hear your words but I truly don't know how to apply them. Can you please send someone to sit by me and be next to me while I'm trying to be still?" Immediately my dad was there. He had passed away, but there he was sitting next to me in the empty theatre chair. In my spirit, I wrapped my arm through his and held his big forearm. I loved his forearms. They were so round and muscular from all the sheetrock he had carried over the years. My dad has a strong calming influence on everyone he meets. I love him. I started talking to him, in my head of course. I thanked him for coming. I was so happy to see him. I wanted to know all kinds of things, especially what he had been doing.

He leaned into me and said, *"Shhh, I'm helping you be still."* Ha! I laughed, *"Oh okay. But it sure is hard not to talk to you when you are sitting right here."*

"I know, but let's just practice. Look up at your daughter," he said.

When she caught my eye, I gasped. She looked like an angel! I could see white glowing around her. She was a beautiful shining light.

My dad said, *"Isn't she beautiful? She looks just like an angel."* We were both seeing the same thing.

The choir began to sing a really fun rendition of "Skip to My Lou." Tears welled in my eyes as my dad began singing, smiling, and laughing. He loved songs like this! He sang and whistled this tune throughout the house when I was growing up. Thanks to the tender mercies of the Lord and the visit from my angel, I had peace in my heart. I was able to be still.

Like previous experiences have done, that moment prepared me to be still at this time. My husband is making some very big decisions. I've been told to not say a word. Let him figure this out. My old patterns and behaviors want to jump in and save the day. I want to try and fix the problem, but I haven't! Yay me! If you knew me, you would cheer for me too! This is so hard to keep quiet and let God do all the work. It's been almost four weeks and I haven't said anything! Oh, there have been times I wanted to. Several times I've spoken the anger and resentment I feel toward him in my head, wanting so badly to come unglued. But I haven't. At times I have literally felt the restraint from Heavenly Father holding me back. I can then listen to reason and I gain perspective. I can see how nothing good will come from me getting angry. Not right now anyway. So I pause, give it to God, and walk away.

By doing this, God has been able to show me other things. He has released me from the need I have to control. He showed me that being still doesn't mean I'm lazy. If I'm listening to Him and doing the work that keeps me in tune with my spirit and with Him, then He will take care of the rest. And He knows more about EVERYTHING than I do. A huge weight has been lifted off my shoulders. This is not mine to carry. I wish I could have learned this one sooner. Line upon line. One step at a time. Everything in its proper order. Learn this, then I'll show you that, then you can accomplish this. It all makes so much sense to say it. The learning and applying is the tricky part. It's a good thing He's patient with me.

CHAPTER 16

Being Broken Isn't All Bad

One night, in the fall of 2014, which was after rehab but before in-house separation, we had a turning point event. This was something that hadn't happened up to that point in our recovery journey. For the first time ever, my husband asked if he could talk to me. He had some things he had not been truthful about. It felt great to listen to him be accountable for his past behaviors and see that he now recognized them as behavioral incidents that led to mistrust. He talked and I listened. I didn't say anything. In the past, listening was hard for me. I had so much to say! I could have spouted off a million things at that point, but I didn't. In fact, I didn't even have to hold myself back. I could feel the work that I had done. It was all making sense and coming to use. I was no longer caught up in the spin cycle. I was not jumping in the pot to either fix, reprimand, or coddle him. I was purely an observer. I felt empowered! I felt accomplished.

It felt good to sit there without a racing heartbeat or thoughts of what else he was still hiding. I didn't care! I was just so glad to be where I was. I felt so pleased that the healing power of the Savior was working. I had been doing my very best working through this trial and He, my almighty God, was healing me. He is "my portion." He makes up the difference when I've done all I can. I am in awe at His grace and mercy and I love Him with everything that I am. How grateful I am that I have come to truly know Him. The only reason I know Him is because He let me go through something so horrible that my only choice was to give up or turn to Him. I chose Him. Even though there are days that I truly do not think I can make it through, I do because God is with me. He inspires me with hope and peace while giving me my next step to take.

That night, as I listened to my husband without saying anything, he kept looking at me and saying, "Do you have anything to say?"

I just said, "No, I don't," with a small smile.

Because I didn't say anything, he kept talking. Because he kept talking, he was able to uncover feelings and emotions behind his actions. He cried and apologized for all the lies he had told over the years. He felt grateful and appreciative of me in his life. It was incredible to see how the Lord works. I had been so busy being sad, angry, and mad, that I couldn't let him feel his own pain. I reacted to each conversation or argument and that took any feeling or emotion away from him. He could just give it all to me and take no blame. By reacting, I had hindered his recovery as well as my own healing. But staying on the sidelines and observing was an "aha moment." I saw how the plan of recovery and healing actually does work if we follow it. It's taken me a long time to get there.

I've been learning almost nonstop since February 2012, but my brain did not want to accept this principle of letting my husband heal on his own until now. Now, I'm ready. My life will not be the same from this day forward. I now know what it feels like to detach with love. I can understand that letting the addict recover without blame and hate actually *is* better. The hate and resentment I harbored paralyzed us both. I feel much lighter now that I don't have to hate him. I feel stronger now that I don't have to be in charge of what he does or does not do. I feel joy again now that I can detach from the crazy cycle and be an observer.

I no longer wish for him to suffer unbearable pain just to know how I felt and what he put me through. I now know that his suffering is just as unbearable, but in a different way. Now I want for him to have a place that he can work through his thoughts and actions on a daily basis without worrying how I'm going to react. There is hope. We can be free and whole. I'm on my way. I now believe that I *will* be happy again. This experience will not define me for life. It will change me, but I will move past the pain and sadness. I will thrive in my life and find peace. These broken pieces are finding place in a new pattern. Each mended section strengthens me. Being broken isn't all bad.

I don't know how many times over the years I have described how broken I am. Finding out my husband is a sex addict was one of the most damaging things I've ever experienced. The person you gave your all to and trusted with your life betrayed you. Not just once but hundreds, if not thousands, of times. Then, to find out things are way worse than you could even imagine brings on a whole new level of broken. You look at this person and shake your head while saying, "Who are you? How are all these facts of lies, deceit, manipulation, infidelity, and perversion associated with you?" How is it possible that I was living with a complete stranger, a person that I shared my life with, had children with, built hopes and dreams with, and shared a bed? I didn't even know him. Not the other version of him anyway. But our spirits have a way of connecting even when our minds can't.

That first night back in 2012, finding him at work with his door locked, should have had me running. But my spirit said otherwise. I was given the most amazing gift of seeing my husband the way God sees him. For that one night, I was blessed beyond measure. I felt his soul ache to be saved, to find forgiveness, and find refuge from his broken mind. For that one night, even though I was in a complete fog, I felt empathy for him and how broken he was. For that one night, I sat and listened as he cried painful tears of regret and heartache. I was inspired to massage his scalp, which always relieves his stress. I almost dismissed the thought because, really, why should I do anything for him at that moment? He was a thief! He stole my life from me and broke my heart. But I listened and I felt lifted as I served the person I hated most at that moment. That showed me that God would be by me, directing my path from that day forward.

The days, weeks, and months following, I did not have those loving feelings toward him. I was so broken that I honestly thought I was going to die. I told him on several nights that I may not wake up in the morning. My heart was so raw and fragile I could hardly breathe. I lay awake countless nights. I cried silent tears and not-so-silent tears. The corners of my eyes were permanently raw for some time. I lost my sparkle. I could hardly talk to people and make conversation with anyone. That was not typical of my personality at all! Usually I walked the halls at church or with friends at the gym filled with sunshine. Even on normal hard days, I felt the light and love of God so I was happy. But that light was gone. I feared people asking me questions or talking to me because I had nothing to offer. The words would not form in my mind. It was like I had shut down, yet I was still walking around with my eyes open.

On one particularly hard day, I had to get out of the house. I had no make-up, and I was wearing sweats with a hat. I wasn't ready at all. That was uncommon for me. My mom had instilled in me to get up and get ready for the day. That way, you can accomplish anything and be ready if someone needs you. Well, not that day. I was a mess. I decided to go to the home improvement store and get bins to clean and organize stuff. If I couldn't fix my heart and my marriage, then I could at least organize other parts of my life. Maybe eliminating chaos in other areas would help.

As I roamed the storage bin aisle, I received a text from my very good friend saying, "Hey, let's meet for lunch right now." I thought to myself, "If she could see me now, she would know that today was not a good day."

I quickly replied with "Thanks, that's so nice, but not today."

She fired back with, "No, I think we are supposed to go today. I'll see you there in 30 min." She grabbed our other friend, and for some reason, I said, "Yes." She told me the minute I walked into the restaurant she knew. How? Because years earlier she too had her life swept out from under her. She knew the devastating effect addiction causes. Later she told me that she didn't even want to go to lunch. But the phone was in her hand and she was suddenly texting. When I had replied with, "No, not today," she thought, "Oh good," but found herself texting again.

The Holy Ghost knew I needed her that day. Heavenly Father knew my two friends had walked this path already not knowing of each other's trials. He knew that no one should be alone in this, so he sent my angel friends. That was a blessing of love and a tender mercy that shows that the Lord our God visits his people in their afflictions. To learn that truth was definitely worth a portion of being broken. As the years have gone by, I've realized that being broken is the best thing that ever happened to me.

CHAPTER 17

Oh, Satan...We Are Not Friends

Lately, I've been fully aware of the new angle Satan is using to try to take me down. For a while, he really didn't have to be subtle or tricky. He could take me down pretty easily through fear. He could mention one thing in my mind about betrayal and I would take that and run. My mind could go crazy with endless possibilities of the "what-ifs." I could do it right now if I let myself. It's an easy trap that doesn't take much work on his part.

As I've committed to healing, I now have so many tools available to me when this happens. It's rare now that it takes over. I can recognize what it is and who is behind the message. I can quickly turn my mind to the things I *can* control. The unknowns are off limits if I can help it. I can control me. I *can* decide my path and how I choose to live. I *can* stay grounded in truth to aid me in this battle. Gospel principles are my weapons. I would never think of going into battle unarmed. This is no different.

This is the battle of all battles! Satan, the destroyer, is on a rampage. He is always heading in my direction. There is no time to take a break. There is no time to sit and rest. I'm tired and sometimes I want to wave my flag and give up. But then I look into the face of death and I stand tall. I call on the armies of heaven to fight with me. I repeat my truths in my head and I let him know he will not win. He still thinks he will. But, I have made it through each attack even though it's not always pretty. When I cut my husband's ties you could easily think I lost that battle. In some ways I'm sure I did. But the lessons I learned from hitting rock bottom gave me more power and strength than I had before that event. I now see it as a necessary step to finish the war and come out ahead.

My truths are things I already know. They are things I have been told through inspiration and things that I learned in 12-step or counseling. Every person will be different. These are simply my truths. I know that Heavenly Father loves my husband just as much as He loves me. He wants us both to find peace. I know that miracles do happen and even though it looks like my husband doesn't get it, Heavenly Father is still doing all He can to help him to see his own truths. I've been told that even though I can't see changes on the outside, there is a lot of growth going on in the inside of his soul.

I know that when I feel any sort of feeling that Christ would never feel, Satan has ahold of me. This truth is very familiar to me. At one point, Satan switched from being blatant in his tactics to getting me in small ways. He's very patient with me. Ever so slowly, he is trying to convince me that I no longer want to fight for my marriage. He tells me I only need to fight for me and that I no longer need to worry about keeping us together. He tells me things like, "He doesn't even do the simple work that needs to be done," or "Look at him. He's falling into some kind of depression. Well, that's too bad for him. If he'd just do the work, he could be as happy as you are."

The thing that has been interesting is I feel happy that I'm moving on with my life. The things he's not doing aren't making me upset anymore. I'm not getting triggered by events or anything! I thought, wow! I'm really doing well at staying on my side of the street. I had total calm and peace. I suspected something was off when I realized I no longer felt anything toward him. The love and empathy I had gained for him and his journey were now gone. I now felt indifferent. That's when I knew something was up.

Let me explain what I've been doing. Every day for the past few weeks I worked through every emotion I'd feel inside as soon as I realized it was in there. I'd go somewhere I can talk out loud to Heavenly Father. I'd tell him that I feel something coming on. I'm not always sure what it is, but I want to talk it out and see if He can show me what it is. So I begin exploring the possibilities. I start with my go-tos. Do I feel anger? Resentment? Sadness? By opening it up, it just starts working itself out. I eventually can identify what it is and then I thoroughly go through it and dissect it. Sometimes it takes only a few minutes and other times it takes longer. Three times now on my way to the gym the anxiety hit so forcefully that instead of working out, I just kept driving. My healing was my first priority. I got on the freeway and I just drove. The entire time I spoke with Heavenly Father about it all. I did not want Satan involved in my head. At some point into the drive, I would be able to see the issue. And when I finally saw it, it was another "aha moment." I said, "Yes! That's it!" Then tears flowed and Heavenly Father worked me through it. It was such a great experience. I'm finding the deep levels of pain, grief, and anger. I have found that sometimes it's directed at my husband, sometimes toward myself, and sometimes even at God.

I was very surprised to learn that I was angry with God for letting my husband be in this dark place knowing he would not be able to get himself out of it. There is no way that my husband could do this alone. It's too deep. I learned then that I was not trusting that God has a plan and that He can see more than I do. He knows what my husband can and can't handle. During this talk I felt a burden lifted. I had been taking on the salvation of my husband. I was working overtime with prayer, fasting, temple attendance, etc., to save my husband. But God was the one doing the saving if my husband chose to accept it. If he followed God, then God would use this trial as a blessing and my husband would be able to help other people and show them that they *can* get out. My husband can be a light on the hill to the world if he looks forward and does the work necessary to recover, heal, and shed this addiction.

That day I had to let go of the nervousness about his ability to accomplish this great mission. It's in God's hands. Not mine. I still pray, fast, and go to the temple. I still include my husband in all those things. But now, it's out of love and compassion for another human being rather than for my original purpose, which was, "If I don't save him, who will?" I know who will. It's the same person that saved me—my favorite person ever, God.

The last few weeks doing this exercise of releasing every pain has been so healing and eye opening. And in regards to Satan sneaking in and telling me to give up on my love for my husband, I noticed what he was doing because I've been working so closely with Heavenly Father on recognizing where I am at all times. Satan was smooth. He told me how awesome I was. He reminded me how far I've come. He whispered in my ear that I've got this detaching with love concept down. What I do know is that Satan cannot duplicate peace. That peace was real and came from God. Satan used false security to trick me. I believed him for a couple of days. I thought, "Okay, I'm ready to be on my own. I don't need him, or want him. He is a fool...an idiot, really, that he can't see what he's doing and that he will be missing out." I had terribly rude thoughts about him streaming through my mind.

I read an article about finding something good in our addicts and writing it down every day. I decided to do this to get me back on track. For two days, I could not think of anything! That's never happened before! Usually there is some piece of love or gratitude each day that I can find.

But there was none. That was the moment I realized that the peace was real, but the indifference was counterfeit. It was from my not-so-good pal, Satan. I took the next two days to work through this with Heavenly Father and I came out with peace, love, and empathy returned for my husband. This has really helped me to see more clearly who I am and what I need to do. I've learned that I really am accomplishing my mission. I am overcoming the pain of this life and submitting my will to God. I want nothing more than to follow his every step. I feel like I'm almost healed.

In the scriptures, it talks about the six creative periods. God asked Christ to go down and form a world in the six days of the creation. Each day was given a specific purpose. Father told him, *"Today I want you to do this. Once you are finished return to me and report how it went."* *He then gave the next assignment. And again he asked for the report once it was completed. This went on for all six days. He then said, "On the seventh day we will rest from our labors for a season."* One afternoon, I was burdened with grief. I felt this trial was taking too long. I couldn't do it. I didn't think I could make it. I felt like there was no end in sight. I had been praying about this when it hit me. This experience is my own inspiration and an answered prayer for me.

I was reminded of the creation as a metaphor for my life. Heavenly Father asked me to be part of this huge task. My trial can be likened to creating the world. He said, *"First I want you to do this specific thing. Once you have, come back to me and I will give you the next step. Keep doing this until your trial is complete. Then, when it's over, you can rest from your labors for a season."*

Wow! That made so much sense to me. It was pretty crazy but it felt true and could see that I was on my personal day four. I was over the halfway point but still in the thick of it. That felt true as well! Trust me, over the past five months since that inspiration happened, I have been in the battle of my life. It has been crazy but I've made it through and have overcome some things I didn't know I could. I've also had principles finally make sense that I couldn't previously grasp. My soul was ready to receive them. All the work does pay off. And within months, I felt even more growth and change. The Spirit confirmed to me that I was now on day six.

I'm nearing the end of my trial. I'm not saying my husband's at this same place. But for me, my heart is open, my mind is clear, and I have used the tools to heal and recover. I know what to do when Satan takes hold and I am no longer confused about my role in all of this. That doesn't mean I won't fall off the wagon and back into the pit. It doesn't mean that my marriage will make it just because I think it should. Agency is still ours. We both still have to be true to our path. If we are, then we can fight this demon together for the rest of our lives. If not, then I have the path that God has in store for me. I am now confident that whatever that is, I can do it! My faith and hope lies in God. I know if I stay with Him and don't give up on Him, He will continue to show me what to do.

Cutting the ties means so much more than just physically ruining my husband's clothing. It represents recognition. Understanding who I am, who God is, and who Satan is and why he's invested in me. Cutting the ties that bind me includes my emotions. I was trapped in grief, pain, anger, sadness, resentment, fear, and so much more. Learning to see things for what they are is how we are released from that prison. Our job is to cut ourselves out of the cords that take us down to that place where we can't get up. It's a place of such despair that we don't know how we will live. Cut the ties that bind you. Release your pain to God. Find counseling, programs, and online help to show you the way. You don't have to be stuck forever. All the madness has a purpose. See its truth and take what you can. Start climbing. Read articles and grasp onto truths that resonate with you. Call a friend in recovery that understands. Share your pain. Being heard and understood is so therapeutic. You will cut another tie when you feel validated through someone else listening. Take control of your own life. Work on saving yourself. Work on healing your soul and mind. It takes time—a lot of time. But there are some amazing things to learn. As you reach out to others who are walking this same road, you will feel loved by so many. You will find your truest friends. There are groups waiting to take you in. There are plenty of 12-step healing groups that you can join. There are phone-in meetings that you can do from home along with endless online materials to guide you and help you through this painful journey. As you cut each tie that binds you down, you will feel the freedom to live. You won't just survive. You will thrive.

At some point, you will feel strong in your healing. You will feel strength in knowing that you will soon get to rest from your labors for a season. Remember that God is your true confidant. Don't be tricked into thinking Satan is your friend. He's not. He never will be. God is your partner. Trust in Him and He will lead you to find joy and happiness.

CHAPTER 18

My Love Tank Overflowed

It had been almost a year since picking up my husband from rehab. Heavenly Father had given us one year to see if he would choose recovery and heal our family. I could feel the end coming. It was changing. One way or another life would be different.

I had an extraordinary miracle take place for me. Never before had I experienced such mercy and grace and love. Never before had I felt the hand of God in my life more than I did that day. The day didn't start well. I was panicking and tried to use my step ten recovery tool that I had learned from the AA book while working the 12 steps for myself. I tried to pray it away. I was distraught because in less than five weeks, my husband could very well be leaving. It had been a hard road. He has not accepted the piece of recovery that is most important—honesty and accountability.

Two months before this, God told me that it was almost time for him to go. He needed to be an honest and safe person, or he needed to leave. The following three weeks had been terribly hard. He hadn't spoken to me the majority of the time and his indifference was showing. He didn't plan on changing and I was heartbroken. In my last session with my counselor, the word "disposable" came up. I didn't even matter to him. All the effort I had put into us could easily be discarded like it's no big deal. I was hurting. It was painful. I felt left behind, like I was worthless garbage. We did EMDR that day, which stands for Eye Movement Desensitization and Reprocessing, and we addressed those feelings. By the end, I realized we weren't going to be left behind! He was the one walking away! In fact, he was the one being left behind. We were moving forward. The kids and I were solid. We had built a relationship with God. We all had each other. I'm not garbage or unlovable. In fact, I am enough and important just the way I am.

Grief rolled in, though, and the next day I was feeling the pain again. I was spiraling in all the "what-ifs." What if he doesn't change? What if he actually does walk away this time? What if he doesn't recommit and change? My heart was racing and I was feeling fear. Then that trigger hit. I saw a bunch of people in a crowd getting ready for a parade. It was 100 degrees outside, so the girls weren't wearing much. I freaked. All the past trauma and triggers came up fast. How can I be with him if he's not in recovery? Will his mindset ever change? What about every other man? Will I be safe with any man? Ever? Luckily, I was heading to attend the LDS temple in Payson, Utah. It was a new temple that had been open for about a month and I was in a nearby city to pick up my daughter from a youth camp called EFY (Especially for Youth), so it was the perfect time for me to see it. I prayed for peace while I drove. The temple was packed! I guess the Provo temple was closed for cleaning so they all came to Payson. I had to wait an hour until the next available session. My heart was racing and my temperature was rising. I needed to sit, pray, and read scriptures. Finally, the chapel emptied and I sat until my session started. For the first hour of the session, I was not doing well. I barely heard the presentation. I was feeling the burden of losing my marriage. I was grieving. I was heartsick. Then something miraculous happened.

Just as the session was finishing, God opened my mind and poured light inside. He spoke to my heart. *"You have kept your covenants. You have done all that I asked and required of you. You are hurting because of another person, yet still you come to the temple week after week pleading for peace and for your spouse to be healed."* Then with love and strength, He said, *"I'm saving you!"* Those words repeated over and over as I felt them from the top of my head down to my toes. *"I'm saving you!"* All of a sudden, everything lined up. It was like all the pieces finally fit together. Two months before I had the prompting of the timeline. He needed to be honest and safe by August or he needed to leave.

The week previous, I had a prompting to tell a friend. This man was a recovering addict who has since served in a bishopric. We both felt he was supposed to be my husband's next sponsor. We were hoping for a miracle. As I thought back to being saved, these are the thoughts that filled my mind. *We are throwing down these great miracles for your husband. If he goes all in and fully submits his will with a complete change of heart, then he will finally have chosen recovery and you will be saved. If he doesn't and remains the way he is right now, then he will leave and you will still be saved.*

This is what He told me: *"I will not let you go through one more round of emotional abuse brought on by the behavior and attitudes that come with infidelity. If he is not going to change, then I'm saving you. No more pain. You've been through enough. You followed me when it was most difficult. It's over for you. You have completed this trial and I'm proud of you."* I then felt the most amazing hug from multiple heavenly beings. I was filled with a fullness of love. My heart was no longer empty. I felt relief.

In a counseling session around that time, my counselor asked me what it was I needed. Instead of answering, I said, "You know me now. You've heard me and know where I'm at. What do you think I need?"

He said the first thing that came to his mind, "Why are you asking me when your Father will tell you?"

I said, "I know He will."

He then calmly said, "So, what is it that you need?"

Tears filled my eyes and I knew what it was. It was love. I needed love. I could not love the enemy and pray with sincere faith for a miracle when my love tank was empty. It had been drained from pride, ego, and the mockery of addiction. Addiction was the enemy. Not my husband. Addiction has robbed me of so much. It had emptied my tank and stolen the container that held love. It was a thief.

Ryan, my counselor, said, "Somehow, though, you still love. I have never met anyone in my life who is such a powerful creator of love. You are someone who has endured so much and was willing to listen, try, and do whatever God wanted."

That was so amazing and validating to me to hear. I did love! I always tried to find it. I always tried to see it in my husband even though he had changed so much. I don't even know this person I lived with this past year. He is a dark, ruthless, cold-hearted, and cutting person. I don't know this person. Yet, I kept going back to God asking him to show me. I asked him to fill my heart with love for this crazy person. I wanted to be taught how to love like the Savior loved.

My next realization came during EMDR. I was bringing up a face that I've seen on my husband that looks blank and zoned out. It represents when he mentally checks out while looking at a girl. Ryan went through how I feel when I see that face. Lots of emotions came up as we went through this process. *He doesn't choose me or see me. I'm so easily replaced. He's easily ready to walk away. He doesn't care about me. He walls up, blames, and won't hear my feelings. I have no value to him. I am disposable! He has no problem just walking away from the family. I'm not important to him. I'm being left behind.*

As we started processing through this, I had that epiphany mentioned before! No, he wasn't leaving me behind. Yes, he was walking away but he was actually the one being left behind. I had a clear picture of my children and me standing on a mound of dirt with our arms around each other watching him leave. We were strong. We were above all this. We had God and we had truth. He did not want our light. He was left behind and we were going to turn our heads to God and keep going in His direction. He knows all. I felt good and enough. My husband wasn't walking away from me. He was walking away from a life he didn't want to live, our life that didn't suit or agree with doing things his way. We only want God's way.

I left Ryan's office thanking God for showing me this truth. I was enough. I could never make someone see this if they didn't want to. That has nothing to do with me, but it has everything to do with addiction.

In the temple all these things just lined up. Heavenly Father had each detail lined up and ready to give in the moment it was needed. He didn't prevent the panic trigger of watching all the girls get ready for the parade. Even though I have the tools and have done the steps to get rid of that, He knew I needed to sit with that pain for a while. I pondered in the temple how my feelings matched the same feelings I felt over a year ago when He told me my husband needed to go to rehab or move out. I had no proof of any acting out behavior at the time. I only knew something was very wrong. As I thought of living with him, I was sick. I couldn't do it. That helped me tell him he had to leave. I couldn't go on with the way things were. In the temple I was feeling that exact same way. The thought of living with him when he had become this abusive dark person was too much. All I wanted was for him to change. I wanted him to choose recovery and choose me. But that trigger that lasted way too long was for my benefit. It revealed the severity of how much I did not trust my husband and how anxiety-ridden I was just thinking about being with him, especially in a crowd of people. It solidified that my prompting had been right about giving him a timeline. He needed to submit or leave.

It was when all of this was playing out in my mind that I heard those words in the temple that He was saving me. He wanted me safe. I was being treated so poorly and still was trying to love. He was so proud of me. I could feel it. He gave my husband every possible chance to choose Him and recovery. He lined up support for him, including a new sponsor. All he had to do was say "Yes." If he did then we would finally be on our way to recovery. And my marriage and family would be saved. If he chose his own way and his own will then He saved me from more pain and sorrow. God's freeing me by letting him go. So now, if he walks away, I'm going to try my very hardest to remember that he's not walking away and leaving me behind, but walking away from truth and freedom. And God is rescuing my children and me from endless misery.

How could I love someone when my tank was empty? That day in the temple, God filled it up. It was pouring out over the top. It was so full that I now have complete and full love for the broken soul of my husband. I can see what God sees. I can see who he is inside and who he's trying to become. I have complete peace regardless of what future he chooses for himself and our family. I could not live much longer with someone who was not living the laws of recovery. Now I know that God won't let me go through another rock bottom, another discovery day, or more lies and betrayal. He's saving me. I made it and I am at peace.

CHAPTER 19

All is Well, All is Well

One of my favorite songs that makes me smile and want to sing out to God that He is my favorite has been sung by Charles Jenkins. It's called "My God is Awesome." It can be found on YouTube. It's the best song ever! The words just sing to my soul and include these phrases: "My God is Awesome, heals me when I'm broken, hides me from the rain. He can move mountains, the Savior of the whole world, and His grace is why I'm living." These words motivate my inner fighter. They bring out my love for the journey, and teach me that God is bringing me out and I am changing. I am letting Him lead.

Changing our brain patterns is an ongoing process, both for me and an addict. There was a point when I found out again that my husband had been lying. How many times does this have to repeat? For me a lot! I needed to learn how to navigate and be confident in speaking truth and boldly stating what I needed in this marriage. All these times to practice discerning truth from lie was changing my thinking. I was learning. I was doing it! And this time my healing showed. I didn't yell or try to save the day. I just observed and noticed. Months before, my husband asked me to block his Internet access from his phone. He wanted me to put in a password. However, I found that he had downloaded an app that gets around the blocks and password.

I've asked him on a few occasions if he had access to the Internet from his phone. He said, "No, of course not." That day, he asked me to unlock his Internet to add something. He threw his phone to me and walked out for a second. I had noticed on his home computer a month before an icon that seemed fishy. I had looked it up to identify it. It was an access-anywhere app that you use on your phone to access your personal computer from anywhere. I knew that he most likely had Internet access on his phone even though he had been telling me he didn't. I felt at that point that I shouldn't confront him. I'm safe right now. He is not sleeping in my room and in order for me to trust him he needs to start coming forward with these kinds of things. I need security in knowing he will tell the truth whether it's painful or not. I can only continue with a trustworthy partner. So I stayed with God in my heart and let it go in hopes that he'd feel the pain and guilt of the lies and eventually make amends. I was no longer making him choose us or recovery. This was completely up to him and his choices.

Pioneer Day arrived shortly after that incident. I had watched the Mormon Tabernacle Choir's rendition of "Come, Come, Ye Saints" set to a video depicting the Saints crossing the plains. I was really taken a back when at the end it shows all the snow. The pioneers were walking and you saw their wagons left behind because they could no longer push them through the snow. As they were walking, the choir sings, "All is well. All is well." I thought about how long I have walked. How long my children have walked. We are almost there. It's looking like we will have to abandon our wagon and move forward. It seems that we can no longer push a cart that doesn't want to move with us.

A year before, when my husband was in rehab, I was prompted to speak frankly with my kids about this journey and the trials in our life. At that point I didn't discuss the details of why he was gone, but only that we have hard roads and sometimes another person affects our road. The pioneers would have much rather been safe in their homes than on that trail. But other people's beliefs and choices forced them to walk a road like no other. Many people didn't make it to their destination. But they did make it with God. They held firm to their faith and hope that all would be well and eventually be made right.

One afternoon I heard the prompting to come up with a devotional of sorts to teach my kids about helping others, staying the course, and enduring to the end. I prayed that I would know what to say and how to say it. It all came together within 90 minutes and was about an hour in length. There were stories, scriptures, and songs. I played them the songs from Nashville Tribute Band album called "Trek." I told about the pioneers and how they suffered illness and death. We talked about pulling handcarts up the Rocky Ridge and the many who got so tired that sat down to rest, never to get up again. They died in the snow. We talked about the family members who picked up their men and carried them in the wagon because they were too sick and frail to walk or help in any way.

So I looked them in the eyes and asked, "Do we leave our family member who is frail and cannot walk, or do we pick him up and carry him up the Rocky Ridge?" They all yelled out, "Carry him!" My eyes filled with tears as I said, "Yes, we will carry him." We will carry him until he absolutely refuses or until Heavenly Father says, like He did to the Saints, "Leave your wagons and go. You can no longer move through this terrain if you bring them with you."

That day with my children was a beautiful moment of God teaching us truths about our journey. It is so very individual. Nobody can force us back to God. However, we are given other people to help us, fight for us, and even carry us at times until we are strong enough to continue. That day I emphasized the fact that we can't make him choose what we want, but at that point, their dad was doing the best he could. He really was doing a lot of work. Sometimes, though, that work doesn't mean we make it to "The Place" together. Sometimes we die on the road because we decide we can't go one more step without taking a break. I don't fault any single one of those pioneers who just needed to rest for a moment. They were tired! They were freezing! They were hungry. In the end, they rested in the arms of their Savior. They completed a job well done.

It was really important for me that my children understood that their efforts in praying and helping and walking this path are for their benefit, even if the person they are doing it for doesn't accept it. They can trust that God does. All the prayers and fasting they have done for their dad are written in the books of angels. God knows that they love their dad. He knows that if they could choose, they would heal their dad and make him whole. I would too.

I'm sick in my soul that this struggle is so hard and so big. He is working with God in his own way, in his own timing, and learning line upon line. I really thought we were going to be the success story. I thought we were going to be the strong couple that healed together. I imagined we would spend the rest of our lives sharing our story with others so they could find recovery in their marriages. What I learned that day watching this pioneer video clip was that we are making it. We are recovering and healing. We are closer to God and our testimonies are stronger. It was my whole goal from six months into marriage to make it. It was my plan in 2012 when addiction became our reality that we would fight the fight and make it! We would destroy addiction and we would come out on top, full of love, holding hands, and ready for the future. It sounds like a

182

fairy tale now. But, it was what I wanted. Now, though, I see that we did just that (all except for the hand holding). We are both full of love for the other person. We both wish we could see each other differently. We both feel like we have done our part. Our paths don't match anymore and we are at the crossroads of going our separate ways and living our lives the way we each think is important. I still hold a space for hope that we will witness as my husband takes a huge leap of blind faith and joins our wagon for the long haul.

Although, I'm not sure what will happen, I am sure that God letting me spend the last few years gaining strength and knowledge is the best thing that ever happened to me. I now know who I am. I became me. I feel like I'm the me that I was before I came here. I feel completely ME. And that ME needs to live in love, service, and with God. My children and I are leaving the wagon behind in the sludge of the filth of addiction. We are going to keep walking. If my husband runs to catch up, we will welcome him in with all the love and support in the world. But if not... All is well. All is well.

EPILOGUE

Just as it sounded at the ending of the book, my children and I did need to walk away from addiction and the marriage ended. It's been a few years since that day and God and His guidance have been with us every step of the way. We have experienced new light and growth and we have come out thriving. The end was not the way I had expected but it was exactly the way it needed to be. I am hopeful that our family, including my ex-husband, will always choose a life free from addiction and be able to find joy and happiness in this life and continue forward learning and becoming who we were meant to be. You can survive divorce. This doesn't mean you are now broken or your kids come from a broken home. All homes have pieces that are not quite ideal. Divorce just shows the world the piece that couldn't be mended together. Stay the course. God will always show you the direction to go.

ACKNOWLEDGMENTS

To all the women I've met along the way that also have experienced the heartache of your husband's pornography addiction, thank you for loving me and being with me every step of my journey. Thank you for walking into those 12-step meetings so I could meet you. Each person was placed in my path at just the right moment. I have learned from you and heard key insights that helped me in exact moments. You showed me I wasn't the only one. We formed a bond that can never be broken. For those who I attended group counseling with, I love you. You will always be in my heart. You know the depths and severity of my pain and walked with me as I found strength to heal.

To my friends who are now my sisters I can't express the love I have for you. You provided a safe place where I learned who the REAL ME was and how to be her. I'll love you forever. Thank you for being strong. Thank you for fighting the fight. Thank you for saying "NO MORE" to being treated poorly and being brave to show others how they should be treated. Your examples save lives. You all have saved mine.

To my family, who have prayed like crazy for us, thank you for listening to what I needed and when I needed it and understanding that sometimes only one who has walked in my shoes could help me personally. Your faith, tears, and prayers helped me day to day and behind the scenes. I love you all.

To my Dad who went to Heaven without giving us a warning, thank you for answering God when he asked if you would help me from the other side. You were able to see more clearly what I needed. Thank you for letting me feel your presence on so many occasions. I'm grateful for the years you lived and for the years after your passing. You have been giving me your wisdom and blessings from both sides for as long as I can remember and your goodness and love has been ingrained in my children. Love you forever.

To my church leaders who walked this painful road with me and chose to see clearly the severity of addiction, thank you for treating me with love and kindness and respect. Thank you for taking sexual sin seriously and following the scriptures and counseling that pornography and infidelity is not acceptable. Thank you for telling me that it was not my job to save another person, that only the Savior does the saving. Thank you for knowing that each person has agency and it was not my fault that my husband made the choices he did. Thank you for clearly stating you would stand by me with whatever decisions I needed to make for me and my family. Thank you for supporting us both by giving us the tools we needed like

12-step recovery groups and seeing a therapist. Thank you for the countless priesthood blessings you gave our family. Lastly, thank you for not pretending you knew what you were doing when it comes to pornography addiction but being willing to learn. I love you all.

To my counselors, Ryan and Jennece. You both have spiritual gifts that you have used that have blessed, saved, and changed my life. I needed you to walk me through how to do this process and how to survive it. You brought me to a place of healing physically, mentally, emotionally, and spiritually. Thank you for taking my 911 calls and fitting me in when I was in dire need. Thank you for calming my fears and teaching me how to change my own thought process and belief system. Thank you for feeling safe for me to give you the honest truth all the time. Thank you for being a part of my team. I'll love and respect you and your work forever.

To the families in our neighborhood that went above and beyond in serving our family with love, prayers, gifts, and support. You were our stable foundation. You let us know that we were not alone in navigating through a single parent home. For fixing things and offering service, we love you. What you did for us and taking us into your hearts can't ever be repaid. You, my friends, are a part of my children's testimonies. I couldn't ask for anything more.

To my children: You are strong souls and I am so proud of your decision to stay the course with God. It would have been easy and understandable for you to waiver but you planted your feet firmly in faith and you held on. You gained so much by living in the truth and not being blinded. Your deep kindness and empathy for others is a result of making it through hard things. I love you more than I know how to say.

Special thanks to my three editors: You believed in my book and in my story. Thank you! Leann Coleman, Becky Harding, and Geoff Steurer, MS, LMFT, Founder Lifestar St. George

To Curtis Bingham, my cover designer: Thank you for capturing exactly what I felt this cover should look like and for the hours of service you gave to help in bringing awareness to this addiction.

To my publisher, Jill Fagan with Silver Torch Press. Thank you for walking me through the ins and outs of publishing and helping me get this out to the world.

Made in the USA
San Bernardino, CA
19 December 2018